# AFTER I WAS RAPED

Urmi Bhattacheryya is an independent journalist based in New Delhi. She worked as Gender Editor at *The Quint*, reporting – almost exclusively – on women and children who have survived sexual violence. She currently writes for national and international media, including the *Boston Globe*, *Globe and Mail*, *Caravan* and Women's Media Centre, on issues of sexual assault, women's health and culture. In 2020, Bhattacheryya won the UNFPA Laadli Award for Gender Sensitivity for her reporting on child sexual abuse.

# Advance Praise for *After I Was Raped*

'What a terrific piece of reporting and yes, art. This book is almost unbearable, until you think of the girls, families and communities who have had to bear extreme pain and injustice. The author draws you into the stories of families who have endured sexual violence, and the systems that exacerbate their suffering. It's a testament to Bhattacheryya's writing skill and honesty that you are instantly pulled into a world of small unforgettable details (such as a periwinkle blue dress) and at the same time given an education about just how ghastly a nation we can be, with our stupid bigotries and vicious hatreds. This book is unbearable and it's beautiful and weirdly uplifting. Read it'

**Sohaila Abdulali**, author of *What We Talk about When We Talk about Rape*

'*After I Was Raped* shatters the silent heroism of survivors – a myth we love to perpetuate. There are no handy markers to understand a post-assault life. A vital documentation that shows a mirror to every stakeholder in the criminal justice system'

**Anubha Bhonsle**, author of *Mother, Where's My Country?*

'*After I Was Raped* aggravates a question society would rather ignore: What to do with rape survivors? What happens after the public and the media are satiated with the brutalized body? Not only does Bhattacheryya give proof of life after death but also of the endurance of that life. Exploring the liminal space between "victim" and "survivor", Bhattacheryya embeds herself in the banality of everyday life in the aftermath, sitting beside the bodies that are forced to adjust to these new identities. She sits with the person who must sit in the violated body, chronicling all the small movements – the subtleties – that constitute survival, holding them up to the light for all to see. This book is both a return to public memory as well as a refusal to being relegated to a notorious cautionary tale. What's more, the sweetness Bhattacheryya provides in her faithful reporting restores the humanity her subjects might've lost to the outside world. Her attempt to give shape to the inherently formless is a labour of compassion that I hope every journalist has when reporting on this issue. Hers is a noble undertaking, and we're indebted to Bhattacheryya for it'

**Frances Nguyen**, editor, WMC Women Under Siege, Women's Media Center

# AFTER I WAS RAPED

## The Untold Lives of Five Survivors

## URMI BHATTACHERYYA

PAN

First published 2021 by Pan
an imprint of Pan Macmillan Publishing India Private Limited
707, Kailash Building
26 K. G. Marg, New Delhi 110 001
www.panmacmillan.co.in

Pan Macmillan, PaPThe Smithson, 6 Briset Street, London EC1M 5NR
Associated companies throughout the world
www.panmacmillan.com

ISBN 978-93-89109-97-9

Typeset in Sabon LT Std by R. Ajith Kumar, New Delhi
Printed and bound in India by Replika Press Pvt. Ltd.

*To Maa, Daddy and Di – who are home,
no matter where they are, or I am.*

*To Adi – who is home, wherever the two of us may go.*

*And to all the women (and children) in this book –
who are creating and recreating their own
constructs of home.*

# Contents

# Introduction

## What Happens after Rape?

*Dirty railway tracks and a scar – deep, jagged; a
laceration on the flesh of her right cheek.*
*Aamir Khan on a wall. The two-finger test.*
*A slipper by the tubewell – flung with might at the man
who raped her. Whispers of revulsion and a husband
who near-disowned her. And the two-finger test.*
*A surgically sculpted opening on the tiny belly of an
eight-month-old, for faecal eruptions. Gauze to wipe it
all up – lots of it.*
*Self-flagellation. Mostly for 'allowing' herself to get
raped. Some of it for still confusedly loving him.*

THESE FIVE SEEMINGLY DISPARATE STRINGS OF WORDS
are what I think of, when I think of rape; and of the five
women I have written about in this book. Where does
rape end? Where does it begin? Does it start somewhere
between lulling oneself into a culturally conditioned
haze – one that legitimizes male entitlement and the
actual seizing of someone's flesh? Does one take dry

runs at stalking before perpetrating tangible assault on a body? Are there markers and metres between the grabbing and groping, the fondling and fleeing?

In a 1993 PhD thesis submitted to Portland State University, Urban Studies scholar Yaeko Steidel found that 'dysfunctional parental relationships can be correlated with the acts of rapists'. Steidel speaks, among other things, of parental alienation at a time when the rapists in her control group were children and 'consequently, they developed inferiority complexes and came to fear people, especially women'. Steidel's study is almost thirty years old, but some of her findings have stayed with me to this day. I find them epochal, almost, of a cultural conditioning that seems both frozen in time and place, and unmoored to one time or place. I think, therefore, of rape that is born in adolescent minds. An idea of rape that begins to crystallize through tacit observations of social mores and patterns of behaviour – an idea that metamorphoses into action, watching grown men speak to grown women in rehearsed routines of condescension. The adolescent mind is prodded to think just as less of women, until finally, it thinks nothing of them at all. I think of rape that begins in impressing upon the crevices of the female body every infinitesimal male anxiety. I think of rape that is exhorted by watching others get away with it.

So that's where rape begins. But where does it end? Media messaging will tell you that it ends in the silhouette of a single frosted palm cutting its way down a glass pane. It'll tell you it ends in a news bulletin about a 'Woman, aged X, raped by men or a man, aged Y' – with aforementioned woman never to be heard of again. It'll tell you it just *does* end this way.

There's so much more to the story *after* the rape. That story can be found in the banding together of survivors; in their disgust at and eventual disillusionment with courts and cops; in the long, interminable wait for justice; in the countless therapy sessions and the ceaseless nightmares; in the changed relationships with one's body and the transformed experiences of sex.

I've set out to trace all of this and more in a book that asks, 'What after rape?' I chose the experiences and stories of Nidhi, Meera, Ranjini, Pia and Smita (all names changed) to answer this question through accounts of their lives. They are by no means alike and their stories are in no way linear.

And why did I pick the stories of these five women?

Nidhi, an eight-year-old girl, was raped by a man she called *bhaiyya*, in an abyss by the railway tracks near her home; the sounds of her rape were drowned by the din of the train. She was four years old at the time.

Meera, a forty-year-old Dalit woman, lives in Dewas, Madhya Pradesh. She was raped because she is a Dalit, by a priest, she claims, who scaled a wall to wage a war against caste impropriety and 'caste pool contamination' by raping a woman who had dared to defy him. She was later subjected to the horrific, now-banned 'two-finger test' that calls for a medical professional to insert two fingers inside a woman's vagina to determine its laxity and whether or not she is 'habituated to sex'.

Ranjini, a thirty-eight-year-old Dalit woman lives in a nondescript hamlet in a tiny oasis of land on the Indore–Bhopal highway. She was raped, she claims, by a Gujjar chieftain in her village, while she was on her period, because she had refused to listen to his 'orders'. She later chased her alleged rapist out of the village with a single soiled slipper, hurling verbal imprecations at him – partly in an attempt to convince her apathetic husband that she had not 'invited' the rape. Medical professionals blissfully and wilfully performed the two-finger test on her to confirm whether she was a 'virgin' or not. In case you missed it, she was raped for being Dalit.

Pia was the 'eight-month-old baby' who lived in reams of newsprint for longer than what was even her age at the time of the rape – seemingly immortalized for the fault of a man who raped her; the doctors had to seal a perineal tear between her anus and vagina and carve out a hole in her stomach for urine and excrement to pass through. The accused is her twenty-eight-year-old cousin.

Smita, now twenty-eight, inhabits a strange dream-like state for most hours of the day – in part from antidepressants to quell the nightmares born out of two rapes, and partly from the ceaseless loop of reliving and forgetting, loving (him) and hating (him), that she subjects herself to. Smita – soft-spoken, diminutive, self-deprecating – was raped twice, she alleges, by a man superior in rank to her at her workplace, whom she was in a relationship with, and then blackmailed, coerced and shamed. That shame – both for thinking of him, occasionally, and for 'causing her own rape' – continues to govern Smita's consciousness and the way she thinks of herself. Today, she calibrates her life by the bruises on her breast that refuse to fade and by the feeblest affections from any man who claims to love her.

Why did I choose these five women with apparently nothing in common except for the single unifying factor of their rape? Because they are united also in the fact that theirs are (c)old cases, with little thought expended on them anymore, since the sensationalizing and the voyeurism of the coverage of their rapes ended. The most 'recent rape' out of these five cases happened two and a half years ago, and the oldest happened nine years ago. Yet, nothing has changed. Smita's bruises haven't blended into the rest of her flesh – which she now views as a canvas that men have used to notch up victories on. Pia's parents haven't been able to shake off the paranoia that a family member is coming for them – like the cousin for their baby – any time of the day or night. Yet, no one cares.

I have often wondered if we care only when there's a 'body'. If the body is sufficiently brutalized. If there were enough foreign objects used – objects that shouldn't have been stuffed into a woman's vagina and, therefore, is enough to incite animalistic horror and pique voyeuristic interest. If there was more than one man, how many men, how many penises. If the words 'brutal' and 'gang rape or murder' are used many times – enough times – in a libidinous cycle of media messaging. If photographs are blurred just the right amount – with enough hint of skin and flesh – make the rounds on social media for people to know there was a rape.

I chose Nidhi, Meera, Ranjini, Pia and Smita because there is nothing seemingly extraordinary about their rapes. Because they were the living, breathing receptacles of a crime, who were allowed to live. Who weren't compartmentalized into the amalgams of 'bravery' we all know and love – the 'good' survivor; the appropriate survivor; the one easy to know and love.

Smita once said to me, 'Most people, when they know I'm a survivor, want me to fight. They don't care whether I'm happy or not. Why can't it be the other way round – that I be happy, whether I fight or not?'

I chose them because they all also serve as important standpoints for the conversations we must have about rape.

What can we do to better protect our children from Child Sexual Abuse (CSA)? In more than 90 per cent of all cases, the perpetrator is known to the survivor (Nidhi) or often a member of the same family (Pia).[1]

Atrocities against Dalit women (Ranjini, Meera) – their sexual assault – are often treated by the perpetrator as a weapon of war; a means to show them their place or the caste difference. These atrocities have become 'par for the course' in every Dalit geography: decades of popular indifference eventually leads to stunned recrudescence – cue the Hathras rape. At the time I am revisiting this introduction, a faction I support and stand with, is up in (intangible) arms against the systemic violence against Dalits, particularly the sexual assault against Dalit women, after a young Dalit woman in Hathras was gang-raped and taken to a hospital, where she died an ignominious death. She was then snuck out quickly and, by every horrified eyewitness account, set fire to in the dead of the night – against her parents' wishes – by a police team eager to escape dominant-caste ire over what a detailed examination of her body would evidently have revealed. What level of complacence over the country's caste status quo and the confidence that no one would dare shake it up could possibly have prompted this? What cold-blooded indifference to the powerless and eager appeasement of the powerful could have led to this? Even as I write this – even as a faction outrages against the ignominy – another faction protests against the targeting of the four dominant-caste men accused of raping the young woman and rejects the 'politicization' of Hathras (read: calling it what it really is – a case of dominant-caste violence against an oppressed caste group). Could there have been a better time to write this book than now?

Ranjini and Meera's rapes are many years old – they've endured the ignominy. But why should they have had to? And why, despite guidelines issued by the Ministry of Health and Family Welfare, and a stern Supreme Court reprobate, does the two-finger test continue to be used in tandem in many clandestine medical circuits across the country, in the hope to disprove rape by placing honour in a hymen?

And what of survivors who do not 'fit the mould'; who do not serve the purpose of appearing as media tropes for good survivors – feisty, bold and at war with their rapist? What if, instead, they're torn between a love lost (for a man who first seduced them) and a self-hate so deep, so puerile that they're never able to recover from it (as is the case of Smita)?

At the end of each of these five stories, you will find a section that lists out the laws that could have helped – or would help in a court of law – that particular survivor, and in this way, this book could perhaps serve as an arsenal of knowledge for you. These include relevant Acts under the Indian judicial system and Sections of the Indian Penal Code that can be harnessed for your protection as a citizen, just as they have been for Nidhi, Ranjini, Meera, Pia and Smita.

I chose these five stories to be part of this book also for it to serve as a mnemonic device – to help bring them back into public memory and facilitate change. By refusing to let their voices die quiet deaths, I'd like to believe that documenting their lives will bring both, awareness (to you) and much-needed public attention (to them). 'For example, the Nirbhaya case that shook the entire country built international pressure on the government to amend our criminal laws. It is a case that is still relevant in the activist and academic space. Making noise about a case of sexual violence, documenting it, writing it, can bring it back into the public discourse,' says Megha Kashyap, Gender Justice

Specialist and former Programme Coordinator, Gender Justice at OXFAM India.

I met Nidhi, Meera, Ranjini, Pia and Smita during the course of my reporting career. Each of them had featured in documentaries, short mood pieces or long-form articles on their trials, at various points over the past five or six years. This book is the sum total of a series of mornings and evenings spent playing hopscotch with Nidhi or her sister, on roughly drawn chalk circles on discarded concrete slabs near a train track. It is the compilation of many years' worth of phone calls with Meera and Ranjini between my home in New Delhi and Madhya Pradesh, attempting to piece together the disparate aspects of our lives to the rhythmic cacophony of car horns in my life and the cowbells that backgrounded theirs. It is the product of coffee dates with Smita, where I counselled her, over and over again, on why sex isn't a bad thing and how she can begin to absolve herself of the years of residual guilt. It is also the result of lunches and birthday dinners at Pia's – often preceding or following trial hearings at a POCSO courtroom (aka one that is designed specifically to hear cases under the Protection of Children from Sexual Offences Act, 2012).

In October 2018, I called out my own abuser during the resurgence of the #MeToo movement in India. I wrote of the time he lay down next to me in my bed, uninvited, and groped my breasts and buttocks, as I was too intoxicated to protest. I wrote of the night at a dinner at his place, when he clambered on top of me and attempted to enter me. I fought him off that time, but I did 'nothing' back then, overridden by the shame of having 'done nothing' between the two molestations, having 'allowed' its occurrence, convinced that no one would believe me – or that everyone would disparage me, instead, for being the 'kind of woman' who got drunk; for being the 'kind of woman' who left herself in a vulnerable position; for being a woman who invited or signalled rape. I cried as I wrote about it and heard, in the bewildering haze that gathered over the next few months, the accounts of multiple women who had been abused and molested by the same man in years past, who were all determined to tell their stories. It was years past the three-year statute of limitations on sexual harassment, but I complained anyway, compiling my story and theirs, and presenting it to the man's workplace, demanding he be made to answer for his crimes. I'd like to believe that these five women I already knew from before that time, and multiple others, emboldened me to change the narrative that I had fed myself. I also understood something beautiful, changeless and omnipotent – that when one woman speaks up, countless follow; similarly emboldened to speak of the time that they, too, lost bodily autonomy.

I kept in touch with these five women over the years, investigating the tiniest aspects of their stories, following up on their legal journeys and asking after their mental health. *After I Was Raped* picks up where most news reports about survivors leave off – it enters bedrooms and courtrooms, and picks up the threads of their lives today, years after their rape, and in the midst of their continuing wait for justice. It does so through the friendships I cemented with them, over the years. Therefore, you will notice that the book is in the first person; I write of these five survivors 'in real time' as I visit and interact with them, and I have done so to help facilitate relatability with the reader.

I chose these survivors because, in their own unique way, each of them gave me an insight into their psyche that I never had before. How does rape change you? It changes you in imperceptible ways – the tantrums Nidhi throws at her mom by reminding her of her rape, if she doesn't get her way; the laughter in Ranjini's eyes that help steel her against her assailants and the inadequate partnership of her husband; in the crumpled shape and form of Smita's shoulders, sinking under the weight of the world's mistrust.

There's no telling how rape can change a survivor – but it is certain that the story of a survivor doesn't end at an illusory line drawn around the circumference of their rape. If they'll tell you – and in this book they do – their stories have many unusual and particular facets – in that they are *survivors*. How do they navigate a society – the community they live in; sometimes, even their own family – who are intent on castigating them for a crime that was done *to* them that they never played a part in? How do they navigate sex with a husband, a boyfriend, a stranger after the incident? How do they re-circuit their relationship with their own body, after they've been made to feel like it's not their own? All issues that Nidhi, Meera, Ranjini, Pia and Smita have to deal with, on a daily basis.

These are important questions and, I feel, the ones we must ask in order to normalize the stigma that survivors of sexual violence still, shockingly, face. Which is why, the societal insistence on – and (many) survivors' acquiescence to – covering up; hiding their identities; telling no one that they had been raped, despite the fact that it wasn't their fault. One shouldn't have to spell out the obvious and discernible, well into the twenty-first century, but the idea that rape is the ruination of a woman needs to die a swift death.

- A family's honour does not reside in its women's vaginas.
- There's no such thing as 'honour'.

I tell Kashyap and she agrees, 'We are taught to live our agencies in restricted ways. Honour and culture become productive categories and rest on women and girls, and hence the stigma surrounding sexual violence against girls and women. Unless we strive for substantive equality, the stigma around sexual and gender violence will be difficult to do away with.'*

While we're at it, I'd strongly advocate moving towards a state of normalcy, where survivors can name themselves and we can name survivors with impunity and without socio-legal censure.

But that's for another book.

---

* In conversation with the author.

# 1

# Nidhi

## I.

NIDHI IS THE LIVELIEST LITTLE EIGHT-YEAR-OLD YOU
will ever meet. She is also, easily, the most precocious.
The last time I went to see her, it was pouring in Delhi –
one of those unseasonal showers that you tend not to
associate with the capital – in the middle of summer.
Nidhi lives in a makeshift jhuggi near the railway lines
of an overpopulated slum in northwest Delhi, with her
parents, grandparents, an older sister – who is nine –
and an uncle. The slum is overcrowded; its houses are
so tightly knit that everytime I go to see her, I have to
scuttle through several small gullies and bylanes, and
hop over railway tracks while keeping an ear out for any
approaching trains in order to eliminate the element of
surprise, before I reach her home.

But Nidhi is always a step ahead of me. Since I
call ahead of my visits, she and her sister will station
themselves somewhere close to those railway lines, either

laying in wait or hiding, and then simultaneously, jump on to my back and yell, 'Boo, *didi*!' Given my usual stasis – teetering on the edge of an emotional precipice, bracing myself for an untimely demise – the 'surprise' their prank evokes is largely unpleasant.

That is usually how she greets me and it was similar that afternoon, too, even as the June rains pitter-pattered on the train tracks that Nidhi and Stuti knew like the back of their hands.

The moment I saw these two, I picked them up and kissed them. When I asked how long they'd been waiting for me, their petulant voices quipped, 'We've been waiting for two hours now. And you told mummy that you'd be here by afternoon.'

As I delivered a string of apologies, I wondered, for what seemed like the millionth time in the past four years, how they'd managed to accrue the infinite bounds of patience required to station themselves on a railway track, in waiting for a seasoned visitor in unseasonal rain, not batting an eyelid. I slipped my hands into theirs and the three of us made the hop-skip-jump across the rest of the tracks to their shack, looking like lopsided, ill-matched participants of a three-legged race.

Nidhi and Stuti's mother, Parvati, was happy to see me. I hadn't seen them for the past couple of months, so it felt almost like a reunion. We shared our customary cups of *chai*, as the two girls and their three-year-old brother ran circles around us, imitating the sounds of the rain on their corrugated tin roof.

She said there had been something important that she hadn't been able to tell me, earlier, over the phone. There had been a conversation about demolishing the houses in the railway jhuggi, and Nidhi's family's house might be one of many to go.

'Some lawyers came and visited us the other day, saying they'd try to stall it or stave off the demolition altogether, but no one here is really sure how long it can be postponed.' Nidhi's mother was vague about the details; she'd never really, in all the time that I'd known her, pretended to care about the nitty-gritties of bureaucratic proceedings, but I could tell that her worry was half-hearted. That she wouldn't entirely mind if their lives here were completely upended and they were forced to move altogether.

I stole a glimpse at her face as she took one long, thoughtful sip of chai, before she looked at the prancing backs of her children.

I knew I was right. Parvati didi would much rather move. She would move in a heartbeat.

# II

PARVATI DIDI IS THE MOTHER OF AN EIGHT-YEAR-OLD rape survivor. She has been one for over five years now. She hasn't made a single decision, moved an inch, voiced a thought or said something even seemingly commonplace in the four years that I've known her, which hasn't involved her new identity. She cannot remember being Parvati, alone. She cannot remember taking decisions for Parvati, alone – a Parvati who once sauntered off merrily, after a fight with her husband, assured – in the foibles of newfound love and new-fangled marriages that he would follow after her. A Parvati who didn't look back; who laughed in his face and waited to be promised a matinee at the theatre before she consented to come back. A Parvati who was keen to make something of her new home in entirely unfamiliar surroundings by bossing around wide-eyed neighbourhood women who knew (and whispered among themselves) that she'd once lived in a 'nicer' part of the city, which wasn't a slum.

She was keen to lord it over them. She was eager to show them, and her then-new husband, the degrees to which her street cred extended, which she had accumulated over the years, haggling with customers in Ghaziabad, perched on a bedstead in her father's fabric store. She was Parvati still, then, unwearied and unyoked by the many names she would eventually assimilate. She wasn't 'Chhoti Nirbhaya's mother' yet, and neither was Nidhi 'Chhoti Nirbhaya'.

Those were the names I first came to know Nidhi and Parvati didi by, in late 2015, when the news organization I'd just started working for, *The Quint*, had picked up her story from a tiny snippet on page 7 of a daily newspaper, and sought to pursue it. They had decided to call the child 'Chhoti Nirbhaya', zeroing in on a name that they believed would still resonate with the Delhi populace that had been shocked out of collective complacency, a few years ago, by a gruesome gang rape on a bus. 'Chhoti Nirbhaya', one believed, might be just the name that urged that perhaps-not-yet-latent consciousness to donate to a crowdfunding campaign that the organization had set up for her.

She'd needed the money for immediate surgeries (Nidhi spent twenty-eight days in Safdarjung Hospital in New Delhi right after she'd been raped and abandoned in an abyss near the railway tracks) and she would need the money in the years to come – an annual 'lump sum' in a fixed deposit – to go to school and eventually, to college.

I followed up on her case, a few months later, after the first reporter (assigned by *The Quint*) quit. I went searching for 'Chhoti Nirbhaya'.

I was yet to meet Nidhi.

The first time I met Nidhi, I was able to recognize her by her scar. It's a deep, discoloured gash that runs across the breadth of her right cheek. I knew to expect it, from the few news reports I had read that had featured her story.

I quickly came to understand that her scar and the abyss where she had been found, had become near-permanent fixtures in her life. Both will disappear eventually (the scar, as she grows older, and the abyss, hopefully in the future, when some enterprising soul fills it up to make a road) but for now, they stay, like permanent orbs in the background of her eight-year-old life.

I remember Parvati didi asking me anxiously, once, when I was visiting at their place right after Nidhi's *dadaji* had been called to court to keep his date and testify, 'Do you think that scar will stay forever?' I had no way of knowing, but I assured her it would dissipate on its own. I started jabbering about the bruises on my knees and thighs from playing roughshod as a child, but I knew I was making no sense, so then I just kept mum. All the while, Parvati didi stared absent-mindedly at her daughter's cheek. As I followed her gaze to look at Nidhi's scar, the depths of it glinting in the glare of the afternoon sun, I knew her mother and I were both wondering the same thing – how Nidhi's scar was a physical testimony to her rape. As if its emotional impact on the child wasn't testimony enough.

In early 2016, as I began to visit her more and more often, I eventually fleshed out all the details of her story and put together piecemeal information from first-hand accounts of the family and the random, abject news clippings. And here is what I found out: Nidhi went to play with her sister and their friends from the jhuggi. She was lured away from the group by a twenty-year-old man, whom she used to call 'Rahul bhaiyya'. She knew him because he'd occasionally spoken a word or two to her and the other children from the slum. That day, Rahul offered her chocolates and a plate of chowmein from a makeshift food stall, which was on the other side of the tracks – to these, Nidhi (then, only four) happily complied. She slipped her hand into his and followed him obediently across the tracks to the vendors, but he didn't stop at the vendors. She was led, instead, into the pit – a little way from the tracks, where people mostly threw their rubbish and refuse. There, he allegedly raped her. Repeatedly.

The man Nidhi had known and trusted, confessed, afterwards when he was caught, to having stuffed refuse and scrap material into the little girl's private parts. He also said that when she'd squirmed and screamed in pain, he had slashed her face with a blade.

That blade had left that scar.

Rahul had allegedly gathered all of her clothes in his arms and scrambled out of the abyss, making off in the dark, believing Nidhi to be dead. But she wasn't. When the four-year-old regained consciousness, she found herself almost immobile and bleeding profusely. She found herself in a place she vaguely recognized, as she later testified in front of a magistrate.

Nidhi crawled her way out of the pit, and then, walking on all fours across the cold steel tracks in pitch darkness, made her way back home. As she stood at the doorway, her naked form silhouetted by the tiny halogen bulb that lit the passageway to her mother's room, the latter screamed and scooped her up. 'I knew what had happened, the moment I saw her,' Parvati didi said softly. 'How could I not? If she'd fallen down or simply hurt herself playing, she would not have looked this way. *Uske haathon pe chot aati, pairon pe chot aati, ya chehre pe aati ... N-neeche nahi aati. Kapde utre the uske* (She would've bruised her hands and knees, perhaps even her face ... But there wouldn't have been injuries down *there*. And she wasn't wearing any clothes.)'

There is always a sudden tightening in her throat, whenever she retells the incident. Her voice trails off into nothingness, before she speaks in a voice that suddenly sounds unlike hers – quieter but angrier, and more resolute – describing how she'd listened to her daughter tell her everything, that night. How she had held her close and believed her.

Their First Information Report (FIR) was registered the very next morning at Keshav Puram Police Station and Rahul, who was absconding, was seized within the next three days. He was held in police custody, while the process of filing a chargesheet ensued.

'Did you ever see him during all that time?' I asked her during our first interview.

'Once. When they called me down to the station to identify him. He actually looked me in the eye and said: "Do you really think I could have done this?" All I know – and this is what I told him – was that my child would never lie. And certainly not about someone raping and brutalizing her. She was four years old! What do little children know about untruths when someone has hurt them?'

Nidhi had bravely picked out his photograph from an array of photographs of men's faces that had been laid out gingerly in front of her, the day after her rape. She was admitted, immediately after, to Safdarjung Hospital to treat her injuries.

Nidhi had suffered a large perineal tear: a laceration of the skin between the anus and the vagina, that required extensive surgery – one that made it hard for her for months afterwards, to pass urine or stool. Even a year later, when I met her family for the first 'follow up', her mother told me she was still applying salves to where the rape had torn Nidhi's skin, and buying capsules for her pain.

I asked Parvati didi once, if Nidhi had ever seen Rahul again, after the rape.

She had shuddered. 'I would never want her to see him. That one time it happened, when she was identifying his face in the photograph, she had started screaming. The nurses couldn't get her to stop.'

## III

PARVATI DIDI HAS FASCINATED ME FOR AS LONG AS I've known her. There's something intrinsically whole and proud and unbent about her. I'm not sure how to explain that, but she exudes a sense of, 'I'm okay if you don't call me and everyone forgets all about me. It's alright. I've done it before. I'll get through it.'

I've often wondered whether hers had been a metamorphosis fuelled by Nidhi's story, or a narrative arc inherent to her personality, which had existed since long before she married and moved, bag and baggage, from Ghaziabad to these slums in northwest Delhi.

A large-ish woman with a rather gravelly voice, Parvati didi doesn't strike you as a particularly imposing or intimidating figure, at first glance. She doesn't move any differently than the whispering, hustling and bustling women who live next-door to her; she doesn't do anything particularly different vis-á-vis the other women (like them, she works as a domestic help in a couple of houses nearby, past the slums); she doesn't have a larger house; she doesn't wear flashier clothes or have infinitely brighter children. If anything, Nidhi and Stuti have smashed a few pipelines between them.

What really sets Parvati didi apart is her raw, vulnerable veneer of nonchalance that is as transparent as it is moving. If she knows you well enough, she will expect little things of you and your friendship – things like visiting regularly and keeping tabs on her and her children, and remembering to call when you said you'd call. When you don't or inadvertently fail at any one of the aforementioned credentials of being Parvati didi's friend, she looks at you askance, the next time you visit, and struggles not to sound hurt.

Her face is a curious mix of indifference and indignation, as she says, 'The children really missed you. You shouldn't be breaking their hearts like this ... telling them you'll call and then not calling. I was waiting—' she stops, confused, and I immediately start to explain myself, taking pains to ignore her obvious vulnerability and the truth in her eyes.

That is how Parvati didi has been in the three years that I've known her. She doesn't express pain easily, except in sudden, uncalculated outbursts that she immediately seems to regret. Parvati didi also doesn't trust easily – although that is a fact I understand – and puts you swiftly in the dock for needing to leave, just as the kids seem to stake a claim on your time.

She also hates asking for help.

One time, when I asked her if I could take her out somewhere, like I did with the kids on a few Sundays, to the movies and then for ice-cream, she looked shy – like she was on the verge of saying 'yes' before gulping down her quick alacrity and subsiding into her usual recalcitrance. 'I'm good,' she smiled. 'You should take the kids instead.'

I know that even that measure is a lot. The willingness to part with her daughters, for even half a day, and allowing them to go with me is a huge ask; her token act of trust makes me feel grateful. But I find myself wishing she was more demonstrative of her friendship.

If her refusal to admit to human frailty amazes me, her sense of equity inspires even greater respect. Parvati didi is simple; unruffled in the declaration of her beliefs, though she will certainly declare them. Once, as she sat in the sun, braiding Nidhi's hair, while Stuti stood patiently in line and the tiniest of the tots, curly-haired Govind, ran circles around her, Parvati didi opened up in a rare instance of personal exhibition.

'My mother-in-law told *these two* today (pointing at Stuti with her comb and jabbing at Nidhi's pigtail to indicate her, which caused her to squeal in pain) that they shouldn't run around in the sun so much. She said it was unbecoming of girls who were growing up to be women.' Parvati didi harrumphed dangerously. 'She said they should stay home more often; that it wasn't safe outdoors. Said that it was fine for Govind—'

I had rarely seen Parvati didi look at her three children so darkly, yet with so much meaning.

Nidhi asked, like millions and billions of tiny little girls do, at some point in their lives when they are besieged by the self-doubt brought on by the haranguing of patriarchal elders, 'Are there differences between boys and girls, mummy?'

'Don't *you* believe it! There isn't a single thing a boy can do that you can't! Not a single thing Govind can do that you or your sister can't. You understand?' Parvati didi tugged on the ends of Nidhi's frayed ponytail for unconscious emphasis as she spat out her words and Nidhi nodded, hurriedly, to express comprehension. 'Isn't that true?' Parvati didi had asked me – a simple, beseeching stare asking for my compliance in her lesson to her children. A lesson that had no strength in numbers in this jhuggi, where she was raising her children, she knew. A lesson that wasn't even believed by her own mother-in-law.

Of course, I told her, indignantly, looking at the girls, 'Not a mite of difference. Never believe a soul that tells you otherwise.'

Parvati didi's fierceness has never abated and neither has her desperation to carve out a different path for her children – one which was away from the jhuggi they currently live in. Which is why, when she talks about the possibilities of a pre-existing legal framework breaking down the line of corrugated tin roofs and thereby, the households inside them, I don't sense any sadness in her. I sense quiet jubilation.

It isn't the first time she's said it, either.

I've heard her say this in multiple conversations, at regular intervals, at various points, over the last three years. At first, it was with a quiet despair, 'I *want* to move, but there is no way I can.' Soon, she'd transitioned to dogged resilience. 'Once I've accumulated the means, I *will* pick up my children and we will move far, far away from here. Possibly to my mother's, in Ghaziabad. It is far, but I think we can make do.'

'Any place but here' is her constant refrain.

One time, I went to meet her close on the heels of Nidhi's last court date. That was when Parvati didi's restraint really broke. 'If that man is ever set free; if he ever comes back here to roam the streets where my children walk and play, I will not even bat an eyelid,' she half-screamed. 'I will take them away immediately.'

That last time, she sounded the most unwavering; like she'd been pushed to the wall.

I can't imagine what it would be like, living like she has been, for the past few years. Metres away from where her daughter was raped. Watching her daughters play, inches from the abyss that Nidhi had crawled out of, naked, bleeding and wounded, only a few years ago.

I knew that Parvati didi had found her own ways to pull through. She hadn't been called to court since the first time in 2016, and she relied only on information gathered second-hand, filtered through the rather suspect sieve of her father-in-law's words – a man whose information was almost equally irregular.

'I don't let them out of my sight for even a minute now,' she has told me repeatedly. 'I wake up early, finish a few household chores and then get Stuti and Nidhi dressed and ready for school. Then I walk them to school, myself. I walk them right to the gate and watch and wait, until they have disappeared down the corridor, into their classrooms.'

I had seen this happen myself, once, when I accompanied the three of them on their ten-minute walk to school. Parvati didi marched in the middle, firmly grasping Nidhi and Stuti's hands, both of whom pirouetted happily and obediently by her side, school bags and water bottles bouncing to a staid, well-established rhythm.

Once Parvati didi has assured herself that they are well and truly inside the school premises, she goes off to her work; the couple of hours of cooking meals and scrubbing last night's dinner off crockery keep her occupied, until it's time to pick up her girls again.

'I'm usually done far earlier than their last school bell, but no matter. I would much rather be early and wait an hour or two outside the gate, than have them wander alone anywhere,' she often avers.

That afternoon, I watched as Nidhi and Stuti were received at the gate with solemn ceremony by a watchful mother; I watched as they regaled their mother with tales of hastily scribbled homework assignments and stories of how Stuti had fallen asleep in class, only to be poked awake by an irate class teacher ('She had to have her name shouted twice!' shrieked Nidhi, in glee) – one of Nidhi's favourite tales, as I inevitably learn.

I watched the trio straggle up the familiar uphill path towards the rail lines, as I brought up the rear. I watched as they looked determinedly ahead, deliberately choosing to miss the clump of grass growing on top of the pit, to their right, like a curtain swaying rhythmically in the breeze. I looked and realized that I could no longer see past the overgrowth to the bottom of the abyss – like I could, years ago, when I first visited, upon peering into the family's palpable flesh wound. I watched as Parvati didi wrestled them out of their school uniforms and laid out fresh clothes for them to don, which they would soon dirty during their playtime. I watched as she turned her back on them to make a fresh pot of tea, then reflexively looked back to watch them gliding down the ladder to join a waiting, squealing huddle of friends.

'I don't like that this is the only place they can go to play,' she told me as we watched their tiny bodies disappear behind a bend in the road, 'But what else do they have? My parents always told me that children must play outdoors.'

Over the years and the multiple visits I've paid them, the sight had become a familiar one: Nidhi and Stuti coalescing into a large unit made up of all the little girls who live in the neighbouring shanties – Parvati didi perching herself atop the rickety, makeshift roof, using a second wooden ladder leading to the top of the house; she watches them furtively, from behind a tank of water.

She needs to make sure that neither of the girls gets too close to the abyss; the abyss is only a few hundred metres from where Nidhi regularly draws squares of chalk in the ground to play hopscotch. She watches to make sure Nidhi doesn't venture outside of the perimeter of her carefully crafted squares.

'But she knows better than that,' she murmurs, almost as an afterthought.

## IV

AS I WRITE THIS, IT'S BEEN ALMOST FIVE YEARS SINCE Nidhi was raped.

Yet, precious little has changed in Nidhi and Stuti, or in Parvati didi and her husband and in-laws' lives. For one thing, they still live where they do, stifling more than a cursory mention of what happened that day.

For another, they still have no idea where they stand with the courts.

When I first started covering the story, I began with the basics. I asked Parvati didi what she knew about the hearings in Nidhi's case and she directed me to her father-in-law, Shyam ji, a white-haired sexagenarian, who looks older than he probably is.

I asked him how the case was going and he directed me to the Station House Officer (SHO) at Keshav Puram Police Station, who had also been the Investigating Officer (IO) on Nidhi's case. When I went to the station house to interview her, however, her colleague told me that she had been transferred to Mukherjee Nagar;

Nidhi's grandfather and her parents had had no idea about this.

I spoke to her on the phone, once, and at the Mukherjee Nagar thana, a second time, and with her help, I managed to piece together a timeline of the case, that Nidhi's family had kept ill abreast of.

My investigations and subsequent conversations with Nidhi's family followed a sequestered pattern:

I would interview the 'external agencies' in Nidhi's case (police officers who had investigated her case at the time, the public prosecutor and legal-aid officers) and then come back and share details with her family. Nidhi's mother would usually perch herself near the makeshift ladder that joined the ground 'floor' to the first, listening and occasionally asking questions to satisfy a long-nursed curiosity, and her grandfather would look at me intently. They would interject to ask for clarifications here or there, and I would tell them what I knew, perpetually amazed at how far away they seemed from it all. How far from all the minute, myriad little ways in which the ground beneath their feet had shifted since the last time any of them had checked.

Sometimes, I was convinced that they believed that time – within their shanty, on the railway lines – had simply stopped still. I believed they looked at their little world here as a microcosm; impenetrable and impervious to the ravages of the outside world.

If Parvati didi found herself unwittingly uninformed and occasionally insulated from the case, Shyam ji would tell me he'd bought a phone solely to hear from the 'people involved in Nidhi's case'. He told me that a woman usually called him on that phone to tell him it was time for his testimony. He didn't even know her name.

'Do you know who the public prosecutor in Nidhi's case is?' I had asked him, once. 'Have you ever had a conversation with her? Don't you want to know what the proceedings are?'

Shyam ji assured me he did, but stopped at a mutinous 'nobody ever tells me anything'. He then proceeded to dismount a large steel casket from the top of a wooden cabinet and open it to display yellowing, dog-eared sheaves of paper that had been carelessly bundled together, over the years. 'It's in here somewhere,' he muttered, as he browsed through countless slips of paper and finally, triumphantly, extracted a phone number for me that he said he'd jotted down, a year ago. 'This is she,' he had said with a flourish. The 'she' turned out to be a secretary, whose name he did not know, who sat in front of an office he could not remember, except for the fact that it was somewhere in the labyrinthine corridors of Tis Hazari Court, where he'd once been.

I promised to look for the needle in the haystack and track down his family's *vakil* – in this case, the public prosecutor who was fighting Nidhi's case on behalf of the state in the Protection of Children from Sexual Offences Act, 2012 or POCSO courts – through the one phone number.

I remember that as I stood up to leave, having saved the number on my cellphone, Shyam ji looked at me beseechingly and asked, 'You will tell me what she says, won't you? Where Nidhi's case is at?'

I think it was in that one moment that I realized that he thought of me as the link between the carefully crafted and well-guarded microcosm of their jhuggi and the world outside it, which included a police station, a courtroom and people he'd never met; people who were fighting for Nidhi.

I promised him I would.

I met Raj Kataria, public prosecutor at Tis Hazari's POCSO courtroom and the vakil on Nidhi's case. She was one of the first women I met, stared absent-mindedly at fighting a rape case, as I went up to her, armed with the phone number copied from Shyam ji's hastily scribbled notes.

Kataria told me that Nidhi's family's testimonies had been heard and documented, and so had those of their jhuggi neighbours' and the investigating team's. 'Only the doctors' testimonies remain,' she told me. Rahul was in judicial custody and the date of the next hearing hadn't rolled around yet.

She expressed hope of a conviction.

The legal-aid office showed me the details of financial assistance that had been provided through the course of the proceedings. They also echoed Kataria's hope.

I made a note of what they said and called Shyam ji to tell him.

This was it, I told him, this was where Nidhi's case stood, three years and eleven months since the day she had been raped and left with a gash across her cheek.

I told Parvati didi, as well, what I'd found out and she
reacted with more warmth. On one of my subsequent
visits, she'd told me about her experience of trying to
talk to one of the people at court. 'I got the number from
him,' she told me, indicating her father-in-law with a
finger, as he smoked a big one underneath us, balancing
his toes on a single rail line.

'And then?' I asked her.

'I called the number and this woman picked up.
She was very rude to me. I asked if she knew what the
status of my daughter's case was and she said she didn't
and could I please not bother her again,' related Nidhi's
mother, 'I told her I was the mother of the little girl
whose case I was talking about and I had no information
and no other number, but this one. She said I needed to
try elsewhere.'

I would later find out that the woman with the
churlish telephone manner was a secretary at Tis
Hazari's legal-aid office and had very little information
to provide, unless you gave her a name she could forward
your call to. However, as the mother of a rape survivor
looking to uncover details of her daughter's case which
she otherwise had no access to, I knew Parvati didi had
been treated unfairly.

The telephone call wasn't what had most affected
her. Parvati didi had tried to keep herself immune to the
court proceedings for some time now, pretending she
didn't need to know, when she started feeling she was
being shunted out of conversations by her father-in-

law. Perhaps, she thought that as the family patriarch, he would fiercely protect all information, offering her little or nothing in exchange for her questions? Perhaps, she was afraid to be turned down and therefore, didn't ask?

Did she know he didn't know much about it himself? Doubtful.

Shyam ji's bearings were always those of a man in the know, even when he was stooping helplessly that one time, over moth-eaten sheaves of paper that he couldn't read; fishing out something he could use – something he could give to me to find things out for him. To Parvati didi, however, he remained the perennial patriarch, hoarding treasures that she wasn't supposed to have; holding answers to questions she'd been dying to ask.

Therefore, I told her. When she told me about the incident that afternoon, when an unknown woman on a telephone had refused her information, I told her crestfallen face all that I had found out. It wasn't enough because it was only information, not a magical gateway to justice, but in that newfound knowledge, she regained some of the power she'd allowed circumstances to wrest from her years ago.

She's still waiting, though. And so is Shyam ji. And their respective spouses. To hear more. I always get the sense that they're waiting for a sign from the outside to tell them all's okay again and that they may go ahead and break down the impervious walls of their microcosm to rejoin the populace.

# V

IN ALL THE YEARS AND MONTHS THAT I GREW TO KNOW Nidhi and her family, I learnt an important lesson – the first in a series of many. It is easy, I think, when documenting a story, to believe that people will stick to your script. That behaviours are unidimensional and that what you see on camera is what you get off it. That all subjects of your story, especially if you love them, are unequivocally black or white. You fail to account for the grey.

I had failed very early on, for instance, to factor into my relationship with Nidhi's family, a Nidhi, beyond her image as the feisty survivor – the precocious eight-year-old of her jhuggi and the apple of her worried mother's eye.

I had failed to factor in the workings of an eight-year-old's mind in the whole affair.

One morning, during a visit, Parvati didi told me how frustrated she was with the way Nidhi had been behaving. 'I thought it would stop after a few months, but it did not.' She sounded dismayed.

'What didn't?' I asked her, surprised. Nidhi had never been the poster child for docile behaviour, but I'd always found her unfailingly affectionate towards her mother.

'When she doesn't get her way, she reminds me of what happened to her,' said Parvati didi with a sadness I had never heard before. 'If I tell her there's something she can't have or someplace she can't go, she'll pipe up and say: "I wish I could go back to that day; I should have just stayed in that ditch and never come home!" She spits that out and looks to me for commiseration. My heart bleeds when I hear it and I don't know what to say!'

I was shocked. More than the nature of the words themselves, I think it shocked me to know that *Nidhi* had spoken them. That she had flung them at her mother with such ferocity, with such little thought for her feelings. Her mother hastened to add that it didn't happen very often and that it was only during very fiery tantrums, but it had struck a nerve.

I think it was primarily because in my almost four years of knowing her, I'd never asked Nidhi a single question – directly or indirectly – about what had happened to her. I didn't want her to have to relive her experience through retelling, or to replay flashbacks at even the slightest provocation from *me*. I knew that the abyss and the scar, both of which she looked at every day, were reminders enough. I had assumed that she didn't think about them anyway. That, with or without questions, she'd never bring them up anyway.

Until Parvati didi told me what she did. It made me think about the time span over which a human event plays out, and the people at its epicentre who need to brace for its ripple effects. It wasn't just one person. I thought of the then-four-year-old and the now-eight-year-old, and her cogent, lucid memory that must have twisted itself into multiple permutations and contortions by now – day and night, minute by minute – that a lay remark to her mother to elicit a response seemed like no big deal. I thought of what it must have done to her,

then and what it must be doing to her now and also to
her mother, to wrestle with its fallout with her.

I thought of an eight-year-old's resorting to apparent
cruelty to mask a bewildering memory she had no other
way to navigate, and I was afraid for her.

Months after that conversation, I stole a quiet
moment with Parvati didi and asked her if Nidhi had
ever alluded to her rape again.

'Not in a while,' she told me and I've been wary of
following up since.

## VI

SO WHAT HAS HAPPENED IN THE RAPE CASE OF
eight-year-old Nidhi, who lives in a jhuggi near a *train
ki patri*, in northwest Delhi, as of 2020?

There have been some court hearings, although they
are few and far between. Nidhi's family members haven't
been called back to testify in almost two years and the
public prosecution team tells me that teams of doctors
are currently testifying – although at what stage it will
all wrap up, is anybody's uninformed guess.

Nidhi was raped in October 2015, almost a full
three years after the gut-wrenching, cityscape-changing,
conscience-shattering story of Delhi's Nirbhaya, whose
gang rape and death ultimately ushered in a plethora of
new laws to handle rape cases better. A week after the
Nirbhaya rape on 16 December 2012, the Justice Verma
Committee assembled on 22 December 2012, to review
criminal laws and amend them, if required. A Protection

of Children from Sexual Offences (POCSO) Act was already in existence, so this committee did not review incidents of child sexual abuse and instead, it brought in new laws to ensure speedier trials and enhanced judgments for those accused of committing sexual crimes. The committee made several useful suggestions to amend existing sexual offence laws, which ultimately became the basis of the Criminal Law (Amendment) Act, 2013.

The amendments included a far more robust and improved standard for consent, among many other things, laying down that it needed to be unequivocal and that lack of physical resistance could not be considered as consent. This also included setting up of fast-track courts, which needed to hear cases on a daily basis, instead of stretching out hearings over months. These trials needed to be completed within two months of the filing of the chargesheet.

(Of course, the committee had also made a vital recommendation to include marital rape under the list of sexual offences committed against women, that needed to be punishable by law. That, alas, fell by the wayside, trumped by a fear of taking on the harbingers of stand pat familial roles. One can only hope this changes in the near future.)

Nidhi's case may not have been bolstered by the tsunami of outrage witnessed in the wake of 16 December 2012, but it should have been protected by existing laws against sexual abuse of children, regardless.

The POCSO Act was enacted in November 2012 to provide a hefty legal framework to protect children from sexual offences (which included child pornography); arguably, its most sensitive and welcome amendment was the means to ensure children were able to have a friendly interaction with the judicial process. This meant various things for both boy and girl children under the gender-neutral laws. Below (paraphrased) are some of them:

- child-friendly Special Courts would be established in every state to hear such cases (in recent years, these have came to be colloquially known as POCSO courtrooms).
- a Special Public Prosecutor would be appointed for every such Special Court.
- the Special Court would allow the child to be accompanied by a family member, guardian, friend or relative, whom the child had reposed faith and confidence in.
- the child would, on no account, be brought face to face with the accused while giving their statement to the magistrate/police, or during the child's testimony.

Yet another vital requirement of the POCSO Act, 2012, was that, as far as possible, the trial should 'be completed within a period of one year from the date of taking cognizance of the offence'.

The entire Act and its detailed requirements can be found at the User Handbook on POCSO Act, 2012.[1]

Under India's federal structure of government, every state is mandated to set up a Child Welfare Committee

(CWC) – which has the same powers as a Metropolitan Magistrate – under the Juvenile Justice (Care and Protection of Children) Act, 2000. It is the CWC's responsibility to appoint an NGO, a social worker – or any person, really – it finds fit, to protect the child's interests during the entire process.[2] Such an NGO, in turn, appoints a lawyer from among its own team, to advise the child during the trial. This means that a child is represented not just by the state (aka public prosecutors) but also by a team from the NGO. It is that NGO's role to provide support to the child and the family throughout the entire police and judicial process – including recommending counselling, should it feel that the child and their family needs it, at any stage. According to Parvati didi, except for right at the beginning, nobody followed up with them to ensure that this happens. It is as clear as day that Nidhi still needs counselling.

Under sub-section 2.6, 'Basic Principles of Counselling Young Children', one notes that the *User Handbook* states, 'If childhood sexual abuse is not treated, long-term symptoms can go on through adulthood. These may include ... PTSD and anxiety ... sexual anxiety and disorders ... Difficulty setting safe limits with others (e.g. saying no to people) ... Poor body image ... Issues in maintaining relationships ... among others.'[3]

Who's to say that Nidhi, who clearly remembers her abuse (exhibit A: the excitable outbursts to her mother), won't allow any or many of these self-destructive, heartbreaking behaviours to fester, well into her adulthood, years after her rape?

Here's a vital question: were all of the requirements of the POSCO Act effectively dealing with sexual offences against children, implemented in Nidhi's case? Doubtful. Her trial, it is not far-fetched to say, seems far from over. Forget a year, this eight-year-old's family has been waiting for justice for thrice as much time. Was she asked to face the accused? No, she wasn't. However, she continues to face what he allegedly did to her living metres away from the abyss she crawled out of, after her rape. Nidhi's family don't have the means to move. So perhaps, larger financial compensations are in order?

Also, here's a thought, though one might argue, possibly too far removed from the legal ramifications of this crime – Nidhi still remembers. Who takes responsibility for the child's psychological welfare, years after, when she continues to recollect and refuse to block a potentially debilitating memory; continues to possibly live in its shadow? The POCSO Act outlines the need for 'Professionals and experts or persons having knowledge of psychology, social work, physical health, mental health and child development' to be associated with the pre-trial and trial stages to assist the child.[4] But words such as 'assistance' are vague and, even if reinforced in the early stages of a trial, often are not followed through to the end, as a case drags on for years.

Besides, what does one do in the case of a Nidhi or a Parvati didi and a Shyam ji, who have less than limited access to information and, therefore, find themselves isolated from such help? The POCSO Act also delineates counselling for the parents and/or family of the child sexual abuse survivor, deeming it important. For someone like Parvati, it clearly is; under sub-section 8.2 (page 44), 'Coping after the child's sexual abuse disclosure', the Act advises parents to 'try not to completely immerse themselves in worrying about or supporting their child ... they also need to consciously set aside time for their own needs ...' It doesn't take a detective to know that Parvati didi's daily high-noon habit of sitting on her haunches outside her children's school, gazing out unblinkingly at their playground, every evening, and clinging fiercely to their very being at all other times, borders on unhealthy. When was the last time she didn't 'immerse herself in worrying about her child'?[5]

And then, of course, there's the most pressing question of all: Will Nidhi remember?

Turns out, Parvati didi – looking across the series of corrugated tin roofs – at her young daughter playing hopscotch near the scene of a crime isn't the only one asking that question.

## VII

**... And that brings us to the present time.**

IN THE MONTH OF MAY, IN 2020, AS INDIA – AMONG several countries worldwide – prepared to burrow itself into the third leg of its 'lockdown' amidst a pandemic, inducing cold terror like nothing else, I prepared to revisit Nidhi's story. What had happened to her since we last met, spoke in person and heard each other out? Did her court case continue to stand quite still – its almost-eerie silence punctuated only by the sounds of everyone else moving on?

I spoke at length with Raj Kataria, who, when I'd last met her, was in charge of the public prosecution team fighting for Nidhi. Turned out, a lot had changed since then. 'On 1 October 2019, Nidhi's case was transferred out of my court to two new POCSO courts that have been set up in Tis Hazari. I haven't been her lawyer ever since.'

That massive change apart, Kataria remembered everything about that little girl, her family and her case, that she'd learned in almost four years. In fact, throw pretty much any name at her and she'd befuddle you with a photographic memory of every tiny fact, location and logistic related to it – an epithet she proudly, almost wistfully acknowledged. 'I remember the name of her mother,' she said, before reciting it, 'and that she has a daada-daadi. He [her grandfather] came to me once, with folded hands, while we were collecting evidence, and said to me, "Madam, you have asked us all these questions so civilly, you have become so involved in our case...I thank you." I told him it was my duty.'

Kataria remembered much more than just their names; she noted, for instance, the importance of the 'chowmein waale bhaiyya', towards whom Nidhi had first been lured by her Rahul bhaiyya. If anyone was going to be a crucial witness, it was him. She told me, 'I examined him. I put in so much effort into preparing him for trial, but he turned hostile.'

It was one of the many pieces that had fallen out of the jigsaw puzzle. 'The victim used to know him as Rahul. He was, in fact, known in the area as Rahul. But he is registered under a different name in his school leaving certificate, so the defence argued that he isn't the same person she accused.'

The months of August and September 2019 were when she last argued Nidhi's case in court. 'In fact, *iss mein* final arguments *bhi ho chuki thi* (in fact, the court had even heard the final arguments in the case). I had made so many notes for the case; dove right into it ... but the defence had introduced delay tactics at the end ... The case could have reached a verdict by July 2019 at the latest, and that should've happened. It's been more than four years since the crime was committed.'

POCSO trials are supposed to be held in special POCSO courts, which are 'fast-track courts', but contrary to what is mandated, fast-tracked cases can roll on for years. India's justice system is weary from playing catch-up with an ever-burgeoning backlog.

In 2019, at the issuance of a directive from the Law Ministry, the country's high courts supplied data to the ministry on rape and POCSO cases pending trial. Both the data for rape (compiled until 31 March 2018) and the POCSO Act (compiled until June 2019) showed that the cases have a time lag of a little over a year.[6]

Over 96 per cent of the total 1,66,882 pending rape cases, in fact, are registered under POCSO.

The Law Ministry said this at the time: 'POCSO Act also directs that ... the trial be completed within six months. However, despite strong law and policy framework, a large number of POCSO Act cases and rape cases remain pending across the country.'[7]

Look no further than Parvati didi's ever-changing blueprint for Nidhi's recovery, Nidhi's bewilderment and her grandfather's stupor of wearied indifference.

Where does the delay begin to seep into the process? 'Sometimes, judges are on leave. Then there's the large pendency of cases. You don't get frequent hearings to present your case – so much so that sometimes, if you miss a hearing, the next one might be a year later,' said Raj Kataria. 'And then there's the defence counsel, constantly trying to stall the process, recalling witnesses who've already testified ...'

Kataria has been here a while – at last count, she had over seven years in POCSO courts, 'I remember when the first POCSO court was set up here, on 1 March 2013,' she said. She was a Public Prosecutor (PP) for many years before that, dealing in cases under the Indian Penal Code (IPC). Between then and now, though, certain things have irretrievably changed. Her nerve for the account of the rape of a child, for one. And the stash of blood pressure capsules to benumb that nerve – daily – for another.

It was one of the first really shocking ones that did it. 'I was conducting a case that involved the father of three little girls – the eldest was twelve or thirteen years of age. Their mother had passed away. One day, the father had come home drunk and started to grope the eldest daughter's body. When she protested and asked her Papa to relent, he told her – "*Mujhe thodi der yeh karne do. Sabke papa aise hi karte hain.*" (Let me do this for a while. Every dad does this.) I don't know why, but just that sentence – *woh mere dimaag mein aise ghusa* (it knocked the wind out of me).'

Kataria recalled playing the line over and over in her head, and trying to grasp how someone's father could conduct as heinous an act as that. 'I don't know what happened, but I began to feel ill. I went on leave and when I visited a doctor, he told me that my blood pressure had shot up. I still take those pills for blood pressure.'

A woman judge in POCSO court – a close friend – urged Kataria to calm herself. 'She told me, "*itna stress leke chalogi to naukri kaise karogi?*" (How will you do your job if you worry so much?) I've listened and my capacity to hear these children's stories is much bigger, but I'm still affected, sometimes.' Kataria could recount countless instances of unloading on her female relatives at home, warning them to be careful about who their children interacted with and advising them to keep constant vigilance.

In court, however, over the years, she confessed to channelling that pain through unusual methods, in order to crack a case. 'I'd cradle two-year-old kids in my lap and hear their stories. If the defence ever dismissed a child survivor saying she was hostile, I would talk to them gently, breaking the ice and was occasionally able to elicit a testimony from them. Once, when a girl was too nervous about recounting her story on the stand, the judge asked her and I into the enclosure behind his partition, where he sat and I wrote down the facts she recited – away from prying eyes.'

Kataria spoke of incidental trauma latching onto the body, mapping itself as myriad physical ailments. It is an occupational hazard she discusses with women Investigating Officers (IOs), 'They face it, too. That second-hand trauma just becomes a part of you.'

Yet, when it is a case involving a young child, 'You *want* to help', came her steadfast exposition. 'I feel like I'm doing something right. Where many other advocates might focus on polishing their arguments, I concentrate on gaining the child's trust and getting their statement. I just *know* that if a little child says they've been assaulted, then my case must result in a conviction.'

It is this certitude that Kataria brings to cases like Nidhi's, often standing between a brutish defence counsel and a terrified child – re-victimized by an insensitive cross-examination. 'I remember an advocate haranguing a three-year-old girl with unnecessary questions and I had to step in to remind him that he was cross-examining a child witness, not an adult. I reminded the judge, too, that such scandalous questions were entirely against the guidelines of POCSO.'

Kataria isn't on Nidhi's case anymore and she hasn't been since September 2019, when it was transferred from under her care, but she'd like to emphasize that she fought with heart and soul. 'So often, I hear judgemental remarks about how prosecutors are failing; about how the police aren't doing their jobs ... but there are so many other reasons for delays; for a case falling. How do we accelerate the conviction rate in such cases?'

There is much that she'd like to see happen differently, but Raj Kataria won't be regretting the years spent in crusading on behalf of the boys and girls who tell her their stories. She hasn't forgotten a single one.

# 2

# Meera

## I

ONE OF THE MOST INTRIGUING ASPECTS OF MEERA'S story involves Bollywood actor Aamir Khan.

But more on that later.

Just minutes before I met Meera in December 2016, at a rape survivors' congregation held for a group of media houses in New Delhi, someone from her coterie told me that she was a 'two-finger test survivor'. I think it was one of the counsellors at Jan Sahas, the non-profit human rights outfit that had brought this team of women to the capital. With bases across the country, Jan Sahas aims to 'eliminate sexual violence and forced labour, and empower survivors of such violence'.[1] The organization empowers and works with Meera and thousands of others like her.

At the time, this piece of information cut me like a blade. I couldn't believe that the crime someone had perpetrated against her came with such a ghastly addendum. The thirty-eight-year-old had been subjected to a double violation of the body: a rape and then an archaic, horrific, intrusive and altogether medically inconsequential test – the two-finger test – that now stands banned in India.

That was how I met Meera and her husband, Vishnu, for the first time and we ended up speaking at great length, having grown comfortable instantly and also, mutually perceptive. I remember taking their permission to record a bit of it on camera, framing the wife and husband in silhouettes, though I eventually decided not to use the video recording for my documentary, at the time. I wasn't sure I had enough of her story back then, and I wanted to begin with just a conversation – without the limitations or occasional awkwardness of filming it.

Meera told her story – of how she had been raped, allegedly by a *pujaari* (priest), who lived next-door to her in their village. Vishnu spoke about how, later, the pujaari's henchmen surrounded him and beat him to the point of unconsciousness, even breaking one of his legs. The programme coordinator from Jan Sahas, who had accompanied them – a woman named Kranti Khode – told me about the two-finger test that authorities had subjected Meera to, and how it had 'failed to prove rape'.

I had my story for the moment, but I couldn't shake the feeling that this was more than just a news copy. Many months later, spurred by a headline that had nothing to do with her (and yet contained enough to remind me strongly of the quiet woman I'd met that afternoon in Delhi, a winter ago) I reached out to Jan Sahas – which had, by this time, become a major collaborator in a large number of stories – and told them I needed help tracking her down. (Meera doesn't stay too far away from the organization's office in Dewas, Madhya Pradesh. Her village is a few kilometres from the main town.)

Ashif Shaikh, who is the founder of Jan Sahas and also extremely accommodating when it comes to assisting with a story, informed Meera that I was coming to meet her.

I was also told that I could be accompanied by one of the organization's field workers each time I wanted to visit a survivor, if I so wished.

## II

I CALLED MEERA A COUPLE OF WEEKS BEFORE I TURNED up at her house. Her husband answered (Meera doesn't own a cellphone) and I left a message with him for her. I had spoken to the couple several times on the phone in the past year, but it had also been over a year since that winter rendezvous, so I wasn't sure how welcome an impromptu visit from me would be.

But Vishnu sounded pleased. 'We don't get a lot of visitors. I suppose we live a little out of the way for the townsfolk. I'll tell my wife you're coming,' he said.

He hung up. I booked my tickets and reached them in a fortnight.

Ashif offered me a warm reception when I turned up at the Jan Sahas office in Dewas, about an hour and a half's drive from Indore. He was delighted to see me, 'You actually made it,' he said. Over the past couple of years, I had followed up many a story that had found its inception in the country's heartland, cross-checking sources with the organization and perambulating various geographical frontiers, but this was the first time I was paying a visit to the people on the other end of the phone.

Manju didi, a woman in her early thirties, was assigned the task of accompanying me to see Meera. I understood her to have been the primary respondent in Meera's case – her 'case worker', as she put it – and, therefore, out of all her co-workers, she knew Meera best. She made that clear on the way, as our car trundled across undulating, labyrinthine roadways that led out of Dewas; small concrete buildings giving way to fields of yellow. 'Didi, if you must take a photo outside her house, make sure you do it furtively,' she told me.

'I don't plan to take a photo outside her house,' I told her, taken aback.

'The last time I brought a reporter here to see Meera, she clicked a photograph on her mobile phone of the road leading to Meera's house. That road included the alleged rapist's house, and he charged at us in a rage, thinking she was taking a photo of his house. It was hard to get away,' she said.

That might have been my first brush with understanding the tactile, very *physical* and strangely, empirical nuances of a life after reporting your rape; of the gravity of not just living your life inches from where you felt violated, but also of living mere metres away from the person who made you feel that way – he, who perpetrated the said crime. For Meera, there was no choice, Manju didi told me. She had to share a wall with the man she claims raped her.

I looked at the house as our car neared it. Manju didi was right: Meera's house, a misshapen mass that was part brick and part mud, abutted a much larger red-brick house with a gate, that, if it was swung too hard, would hit the neighbours in the face. This, as I understood from my companion's nod, was where Jeevan, the pujaari and Meera's alleged rapist lived.

## III

MEERA SHUFFLED AROUND THE EARTHEN PERIMETER OF her home, offering an eager tour while Manju didi, who had already been here multiple times during the course of her interrogations, took a seat at the foot of Meera's cot – the only tangible piece of furniture they had in their one-room living space.

I was surprised to see a thin, blue tarpaulin sheet – instead of a solid wall – serving as the only defence against the elements along the back edge of Meera's cottage. 'Don't you get snakes and reptiles in the monsoon?' I asked. 'Yes,' she told me, 'but we never even had a sheet before.' She'd put this one up, she told me, the day after Jeevan accosted her in her own backyard.

Meera could remember walking to the fields to relieve herself, one evening, weeks after her rape; the subsequent police custody of Jeevan and his eventual release. 'He was waiting for me right there,' she said, pointing to a gap between two sizable hedges. 'I had barely lifted my saree, tiptoeing on my haunches, when he towered over me and threatened that I take back my complaint. "Sign a *maafinama* (a letter of acknowledgement/atonement of/for a crime or injury done to another) and accept twenty-five thousand rupees from me; consider that the end of all this trouble," he told me. But I don't know what got into me that day. I shouted "No!" and ran back to my house. I wasn't afraid of him anymore.'

Meera's fear, even for her, was a memory, but one she could remember vividly, almost palpably, as she painted me a word-picture. We whispered, because as she told my companion and me, she couldn't risk her voice travelling across the wall to him and his family, lest the latter stirred up fresh trouble.

'I remember the fear I felt when I first felt his hands on me,' she said, and pointed to a spot a few inches away from where we were sitting, at the foot of her cot. 'I sleep there, on a mattress on the floor. It was where I was sleeping that night.'

Meera was alone on the night of 9 May 2011 – her husband and her three sons had left for a wedding, earlier that day. 'My brother's daughter was getting married, so the men in the family had gone to "fetch" the groom. It's a tradition in our parts.'

She had been sleeping only a few hours, when she felt a hand clamp down on her mouth. 'He must have entered through the back,' she recalled. 'There was no doorway to speak of.' Meera immediately knew who it was. She had been seeing his face, contorted in rage, and hearing his voice, garbled in anger and contempt, for a year since the family moved into the house. He wasn't happy, she recalled, that a *neech jaati* (someone from 'a lower caste') was going to be living in such close proximity to him, upending the foundations of his perfectly compartmentalized life. '*Woh oonche jaati ke hai* (he belongs to a higher caste),' she offered by way of explanation, introducing into the conversation the vagaries of privilege that the paradigmatic and utterly discriminatory Hindu caste system accorded to its constituents. 'But we had worked hard to earn our way into this house. Why should we have to move away?'

The bitter feud, fuelled by the occasional hurling of verbal imprecations across the wall and whenever Meera's family went to the village temple where Jeevan officiated, continued for a year – culminating in the night he allegedly visited her at the house.

'I woke up to feel his hand on my mouth and I struggled to get free. He began to hoist up my clothes. I used to sleep with a scythe under my pillow and I frantically got hold of it to use against him.'

Her attacker, however, was allegedly too quick for Meera and he pinned the arm that had grabbed hold of the scythe, causing her to press down on the blade and bleed profusely. Meera cried out, but her cries were stifled under the hand that muzzled her face.

She screamed and continued to hit back, until he allegedly wrested the scythe from her and hit her on the head with its blunt end. Meera could, in her copious retelling of the story, remember two things: the cold, sick sensation of utter powerlessness and the smell of warm, fresh blood pouring out of the wound on her forehead, where the scythe had hit her.

It was a deep cut, and it blinded her. By this time, Meera had stopped struggling and Jeevan had allegedly stopped raping her.

'I don't know where I summoned the energy after that, but I did – just enough to run out of the house like a madwoman. I could hear him shout after me and then shout out to his henchmen in the village to stop me, but I didn't look back. I didn't stop. I kept running across the fields in pitch darkness. I remember wondering later how I could have remembered to put my *chappals* on,' said Meera.

Meera didn't stop until she reached a thana in Dewas district, where she half-collapsed on the steps. She remembered it being close to 3 a.m. when she stumbled in and told the cops what had happened and that she wanted to file an FIR.

'All night I waited. I remember there were three cops at the time – I remember that part vividly – and they just heard my story indifferently and asked me to wait on the bench until they could call me in. I sat on the cold hard bench outside one of the sub-inspectors' rooms, holding my bleeding head in my hands.'

None of the policemen present, Meera said, tended to her injuries or asked her if she wanted anything.

'I kept pleading with them – any time one of them passed by me – to write out my complaint; I told them that I was alone and that the men could catch up with me any time, but no one seemed to hurry or listen to my plea.'

Meera's fears weren't unfounded, however, as according to her, Jeevan's brother and a few of his friends soon reached the police station, looking for her. 'They didn't enter; perhaps, they were scared. But they taunted me from outside and spoke loudly enough among themselves for me to hear: "She has come to the cops. If we had waylaid her on the road, we could have killed her."'

The men left soon after, but no one came for Meera. Soon, it was daybreak and she could remember more cops pouring in, some with *chai* and *naashta* for the rest of the men, chattering and milling around, not throwing so much as a second glance at her.

While Meera sat there and bled, trying to stem the force of the blood with her hands, the cops reportedly dawdled and ate their meals, and finally called her in to file her FIR a little past 9 a.m. It was while she was recounting the events of the night that her husband walked in.

'Some of our neighbours who had seen and heard what was happening filled him in when he returned from the groom's house, and he immediately came down to the police station to find me,' she said.

Till date, Meera hasn't forgotten or forgiven her neighbours for not coming to her aid. 'How can it be that no one heard anything? We live in *kuchcha* houses and sound carries easily. Even if they didn't hear anything, they must have seen me running away from my own house!' she often asks in anguish.

## IV

IT WAS 12 P.M., WHEN THE COPS FINALLY SENT HER TO the district hospital for her medical examination, post the filing of her FIR. The date and time stamp are imprinted on the Medico-Legal Certificate (MLC) issued by the hospital – that I accessed and studied. Her husband went with her. Here, the ordeal continued.

'There were two female doctors who had been assigned the task of my "medical", but once they'd caught a glimpse of me, they seemed least interested in rushing to help me. They said I would have to wait a while and I told them that was fine, but could I please get something for my bleeding forehead and hand meanwhile? But they paid no heed,' said Meera.

When she was finally called in, she said she was attended to by the resident physician (the woman with her was 'some sort of trainee', she believes).

'The doctor tested me indifferently and at various points through the exam, kept asking me if I was sure I was raped. She probed and she poked, and I kept

wincing in pain and telling her, "Why would I lie?"'
Meera, at this point, had no idea what she had just
been subjected to; that the doctor, probing her insides
had just, unbeknownst to the survivor, committed an act
which was mere months away from becoming a crime;
a casual violation of her body. She was told only weeks
later, when Jan Sahas caught up with her to instruct her
on court practices, that the hospital had conducted a
two-finger test – also known as a PV (Per Vaginal) – a
medically unnecessary scoping of the vagina to check
whether the hymen is distensible or not.

The two-finger test, by every definition – in particular
in the one given by Human Rights Watch, an international
non-governmental organization that 'conducts research
and advocacy on human rights'– is a 'practice where the
examining doctor notes the presence or absence of the
hymen and the size and so-called laxity of the vagina of
the rape survivor, to assess whether girls or women are
"virgins" or "habituated to sexual intercourse".'[2] Why
was this test (now banned in India) even conducted?

I have looked at a hard copy of Meera's medical
examination and the first thing that caught my eye,
before I read the details of the test, were the two cents
of personal information that she had been asked for.
Next to 'name' and 'address', is a column for 'jaati' or
caste, where Meera and Vishnu have been classified as
'Chamar' (or Dalits). Why is such an assignation or
epithet deemed necessary by an examination that is
meant to collect forensic evidence of rape?

Below her personal information and details of samples and clothes sent for further forensics, Meera's medical superintendent (the designation mentioned in her test) has scribbled the word 'Opinion'. Next to this, she writes: 'No definite opinion can be given regarding sexual intercourse since she is habituated for (sic) it.'

I deviate here, slightly, from Meera's first-hand account of the incident, but days after I returned from Dewas, I spoke to Dr Kaminidevi Bhoir, Honorary Psychiatry Counsellor for Mumbai Police, for a story I was writing on the two-finger test and the protocol one needed to know after rape. I asked her about medical tests and what one should do if they are menstruating at the time of the test – according to Meera's report and even by her own account, she had been on her period at the time. Dr Bhoir said: 'If a woman is menstruating, the best recourse is to call her back at a second date for a re-examination. Samples can be found in the body even a week after assault.'[3]

In a conversation with me in early 2021, Dr Bhoir added, 'During that time, courts actually wanted to abolish the two-finger test. With regards to the regular medical examination, there is a high chance of finding the most evidence should the exam be done right after the rape. However, debris of sperm may remain in the vaginal passage for around a period of one week. Menstrual flow, though, will wash out all evidence irrespective of sperm count.'

Although Meera's exam was conducted within twenty-four hours of her rape, certain factors, such as whether the examinee is menstruating at the time of the rape, whether the assailant ejaculated at the time of rape or whether he has a low sperm count, are all factors that can affect the results of a test. *The Medical Examination of Survivors/Victims of Sexual Violence: A Handbook For Medical Officers* published by United Nations Fund for Population Activities (UNFPA), the Public Health Department and National Health Mission (NHM) contain this useful piece of information:

> It is always wise to collect whatever evidence is available at the time of medical examination even if the woman is menstruating. There are always chances of losing trace evidences in cases of heavy menstrual blood flow occurring at the time of assault, as well as at the time of medical examination ... If a woman is menstruating at the time of collection of medical evidence then a repeat medical examination is warranted.[4]

On the issue of ejaculation, the handbook states that when a doctor is asked during testimony in the course of a rape trial whether he/she could say it was a case of rape/sexual assault in the absence of semen, he/she should say:

> Semen may not be found in the following cases ... Penile penetration but ejaculation did not occur ... Penile penetration but ejaculation occurred outside the body ... Penile penetration but a condom was used and was not recovered ... The accused was azoospermic

... There is inordinate delay between the commission of sexual violence and medical examination that even if spermatozoa were present at the time of sexual violence – they would have disintegrated and are beyond recognition.

(The compilation/handbook is 'an outcome of a series of capacity building programs on Health sector response to violence against women and medico-legal care of survivors of sexual violence, organized for Civil Surgeons, Medical Superintendents and Gynaecologists from District and Sub- District hospitals of Maharashtra'. It asks to be used 'together with the MOHFW Guidelines and Protocols for medico- legal care for survivors/victims of sexual violence, 2014.')[5]

Meera's period, at the very least, called for a second examination. However, none was conducted.

A doctor, after having attended to a rape survivor, is mandated to release an MLC that becomes part of the evidence. This is usually accompanied by forensic evidence such as sealed samples of vaginal swabs, blood samples, nail clippings and so on, which is then handed over to the police. The police takes these samples to a forensic laboratory to prepare a final report to be presented as evidence in court.

I often ask myself, as do several doubters of the single medical examination (in Meera's case, of course, even more dubious because of the inclusion of the two-finger test) what happens if the survivor did not struggle? If she froze and, therefore, made it difficult for the assailant to leave physical injury or signs of abrasion on her vagina? If she did not scratch him, and therefore, left no nail clippings? If the assailant did not bite or lick her, and therefore, left no other evidence on her body?

What the two-finger test does is judgementally and peremptorily plant the idea of consent between 'rapist' and 'rape survivors', and sometimes, the presumption of consent is all it takes to shake the foundations of a rape case.

In November 2017, Human Rights Watch released an extensive report that documented twenty-one cases of sexual assault, interviews with more than fifteen lawyers, civil society workers and advocates, as also twelve government officials (including seven serving police officials) across four states – Madhya Pradesh, Haryana, Uttar Pradesh and Rajasthan – from December 2016 to August 2017. 'These four states were chosen because of large numbers of rape cases reported from them, and the presence of strong local non-governmental organizations that could facilitate access to legal, medical, and police documents. Interviews were also conducted in the cities of New Delhi and Mumbai.'[6]

An earlier report published by HRW in 2010, noted:

Indian criminal law does not require corroboration by forensic evidence to secure a conviction for rape, yet in practice, such evidence plays a critical role. Lawyers and activists say that the seriousness with which police investigate a complaint of rape usually depends on the manner in which a doctor collects and reports forensic evidence, and judges frequently give this evidence significant weight. A rape survivor ... may see the perpetrator walk free if the evidence was improperly collected, stored, or reported.[7]

This is exactly what happened in Meera's case.

## V

MEERA WAS RAPED ON THE INTERVENING NIGHT BETWEEN 8 and 9 May 2011. She fought her case for a period of over two years, until judgment was pronounced on 4 October 2013. The Dewas district court gave her alleged rapist the benefit of doubt and allowed him to walk free. The fact that medical evidence was inconclusive, posed the biggest obstacle in her case, Ashif Shaikh believes.

He told me later: 'The case relied heavily on forensic evidence, even though it had included the terrible two-finger test. Even the trial itself wasn't fair – I attended a few hearings. One time, the judge kept mentioning over and over again how Vishnu had not been at home on the night of the rape. He kept saying, "but a wedding is a woman's responsibility. Why was Meera even at home that night, while her husband and sons were not?" Her character was questioned.'

It was something Meera herself remembered with indignation as we sat, cross-legged, opposite one another on the earthen floor of her Dewas home. 'Men always go to get the groom in our community. That's how it has always been. How could I have helped the fact that my husband wasn't home?'

However, that wasn't the most unfortunate part of her trial. The judgment, ironically, came just five months – in May 2013 – after the Supreme Court held that the two-finger test violates a woman's right to privacy, and asked the government to provide better medical procedures to confirm sexual assault. A bench of Justices B. S. Chauhan and F. M. I. Kalifulla, said, 'Undoubtedly, the two-finger test and its interpretation violates the right of rape survivors' privacy, physical and mental integrity and dignity. Thus, this test, even if the report is affirmative, cannot ipso facto, be given rise to presumption of consent.'[8]

It was a little too late for Meera.

'If I'd known what tests they were conducting, I would have said no,' she told me that afternoon in the precarious safety of her home, but as Manju didi interjected, 'That would've been hard, considering that the consent for a medical examination is usually taken as a whole, instead of being sought for each component separately.'

Some good news followed for sexual assault survivors in the wake of the Supreme Court ruling. In 2014, India's Ministry of Health and Family Welfare issued guidelines for better medico-legal care for those who have been sexually assaulted. These guidelines eliminated the abhorrent two-finger test. The guidelines were adopted by nine states in India – Madhya Pradesh, Meera's home state, was one of them.

Incidentally, other states which didn't adopt the 2014 central government guidelines do have their own specifications, but they are nowhere near as detailed and sensitive as the 2014 ones. Of course, adoption is hardly equivalent to implementation – as Meera's case shows, so very well.

If her trial resulted in heartbreak, things at home regressed from bad to worse. Within weeks of Meera having filed her FIR and then refusing to withdraw it (post his accosting her in the fields), Meera alleged that he sent goons to bash up her husband. 'What was funny was that those men had no idea what they were getting into,' she told me, in wonder. 'They beat him up black and blue – almost to the point of unconsciousness – and he lost the function of his leg for several months. However, he (my husband) hardly fought back, and when they were satisfied they'd beaten him enough, he somehow sat up and told them what had happened to his wife. They apologized to him profusely, but what was done was done.'

With Vishnu out of action for months and her children too young at the time to work, Meera willingly took up the succour and employment that came her way from Jan Sahas. 'They' – she fondly looked at Manju didi as she said this – 'gave me a sewing machine and a month of classes. I started stitching blouses for the ladies nearby. I can make so many things now! Look!'

I looked, as Meera got off of her haunches, and gingerly brought down shimmering pieces of blue, gold and silver – blouses and *cholis* in various stages of embroidery that she had been poring over adoringly for months. I fingered the silken material, marvelled aloud at the necklines and she blushed and said she'd been trained to stitch Patiala suits too, but had forgotten now.

What are Meera's chances today? She has filed an appeal in Madhya Pradesh High Court, and that has continued for the past three years, with no immediate silver lining in sight.

Meanwhile, Jeevan, she says, has been perambulating the circumference of Meera's tiny house for seven whole years now, a free man, occasionally hollering across the wall to 'guests' about how ill-willed agents tried to act against him in the past, but how he managed to emerge unscathed.

'Sometimes, when I sit at our tea shop in front of the house, I'll hear him tell others loudly, "*Main toh jeet gaya*",' Meera recalled, looking down at her feet and starting to scuff at one of her toes. It is a symptom of restlessness that she displays, in constant, repetitive loops of time.

What must it feel like, living next door to the man you said raped you, and have him announce to the world at large and your own auditory pleasure, that you have, in fact, been too powerless to keep him locked up? Just as powerless as you felt on the first night he walked in, uninvited?

# VI

BY THIS TIME, WE HAD FINISHED OUR SECOND CUP OF milky, sugary tea and Meera, Manju didi and I had descended into sudden, not-so-uncomfortable silence. It was at this point that I looked up at the wall directly opposite me and the piece of paper adorned in a gilded frame; I'd been eyeing the letter for a while, especially since I'd known what it was, the second I'd stepped in; my memory jogged back to the first time Meera and Vishnu had told me proudly of their meeting with Bollywood actor Aamir Khan.

'He invited us to appear on an episode of *Satyameva Jayate* in 2014. When he met us, he said he couldn't imagine how brave we were being,' Vishnu had gushed proudly at the Constitution Club in Delhi, where I had first met them, at the rape survivors' congregation.

The Aamir Khan-fronted social reality television show was a pleasant surprise on primetime TV at the time the episode was featuring stories of sexual violence from across the country, under the banner 'Fighting Rape' during that particular season of its runtime. Meera said she was happy to go on the show, when Jan Sahas told her she had been approached.

'I told him that I like him very much when I first met him,' she giggled. 'He then asked me what I liked about him, and I replied "Your movies". I now wish I'd said something smarter then. When he wanted to know what movies I'd liked him in, I said *Mela*. I'd only just seen *Mela* on television,' Meera admitted with a grin.

I have seen Meera's episode of *Satyameva Jayate* – the channel, of course, blurred her and her husband's faces – and I was immensely moved by the way Aamir Khan had asked his questions – incisive but sensitive.

'He wrote me this letter, right before we were leaving,' Meera explained as I took it off its hinges. 'He wrote it in Hindi; he told me, "My Hindi isn't great, but I'm going to try this."'

I found myself agreeing with Aamir. The handwriting was childlike – words scrawled luxuriously on paper; thick and big; hardly legible. It expounded, in great detail, how brave Meera had been for coming on his show and thanked her for the appearance. It also ended with the salutation, 'Satyameva Jayate!'

Aamir Khan's letter to Meera is one of the few pieces of decor in her house; the other, a cobwebbed photograph in a wooden frame that must have graced her walls for at least a decade, without any semblance of human touch. I asked Meera about it and watched her face visibly alter.

'Those are my parents,' she said, as we took the painting off its hinges for a couple of minutes to study the rather stern-looking gentleman and petite-framed woman in it. Fingers caked in dust, Meera traced the harmonium on her father's lap – the duo were seated on a wooden bench, with their backs to what I suspected had been a Chroma screen, substituted by an artificial-looking expanse of green meadows and periwinkle blue sky.

Her father sat with his knees jutting out, an enormous man with a turban on his head and a moustache possibly larger than the one Aamir Khan was sporting in *Mangal Pandey: The Rising* (I should've asked Meera what she'd thought of that film). Her mother looked diminutive next to him – most of her visage was cloaked behind a traditional *ghunghat* and her feet were dangling inches off the Chroma floor.

Was Meera also taught the harmonium? I asked her eagerly. She wasn't.

'He didn't care much for my education – or possibly, very much about me. I went to school till about the fourth standard, before he withdrew me. There was much to do at home, he had said – the farm work; the milking of cattle; the bustling to the *haat* (the village market) to sell our produce. He definitely didn't want me learning the harmonium on top of all that!' she laughed.

Meera had just the toothiest grin. Her face lit up at each pause and each interjection in her story, as if to punctuate it. At one point, she asked for my phone number, 'I know my husband has it, but I'd like to keep it too, just in case,' she told me. I scribbled it on a piece of paper torn from my notebook and handed it to her, and for the whole time that we were there, she kept absent-mindedly curling the jagged corners of the paper and tearing little strips off it.

I was soon to realize that Meera's restlessness stemmed from the urgency to ensure that our voices didn't carry – not merely to the pujaari and his kin, next door, but also to her sons. 'They are much older now than they were at the time of the *kaand* (Meera, like many other survivors I have met, tends to use this word to refer to her rape) and we have shielded them from it so far.'

I found this information rather amazing. Had they never wondered why such animosity existed between the families?

'They'd asked a couple of times,' Meera explained, but their mother and father had chalked it down to a land dispute and that had satisfied the trio.

'But now I keep worrying that they'll get to know what the pujaari did to me and act on revenge. *Garam khoon hai pata nahi kya kar de* (they're young and hot-blooded, I don't know what they'll do).'

For Meera, there are two battles – inextricably linked – one to win her court appeal against Jeevan and the other, to keep her three sons completely in the dark about the biggest battle in her life.

## VII

THERE WAS SOMETHING ABOUT MEERA THAT TRULY arrested me. She exuded the fiercest strength in her quietest of voices – while she stayed, for much of the conversation, with her eyes glued to the floor and her fingers rubbing frayed bits of paper; she looked up every now and then, to share with me a random fact of her life that she seemed eager to get off her chest. Facts about her husband, for instance.

I'd wondered – in no small measure, ever since I'd met Meera and Vishnu together at the survivors' conference – how they did *this*. This sticking together, this finishing each other's sentences when one trailed off mid-interview, this doing it for nine and a half years with no visible signs of weariness.

Manju didi, Kranti, Ashif, back at Jan Sahas, and various other social workers along the way had told me how viciously, insidiously and painfully sexual violence could gnaw and tear up couples. I had seen ensuing blame-games cyclically and systematically breaking people up.

But when I spoke to Meera, that afternoon, I didn't want to ask her any of that. I didn't want to ask her clinical questions about what rape did to a relationship, because her parameters were hers alone and not meant to be juxtaposed to other relationships.

I didn't want to ask her about the instances where they'd talked about the rape; I asked, instead, of the number of conversations they'd had outside of it. Whether any were possible. What those conversations were about. Whether it was easy to slip back into the delight of mundanity and routine. Whether their routine – developed for days and years before the rape happened – helped them return to normalcy. Whether their routine – of buying a roll of *sabzi*, cooking a pot of *bhindi*, reprimanding a son, counting rupee notes and coin piles at the tea shop they jointly own, at the end of a day's work – gets them through.

What did she like doing with her husband, for instance?

She'd never been to a theatre to watch a film in all her life, she said in answer to my question. 'Does he take you out?' I persisted and she grinned.

'Yes, when I ask for things to buy or eat,' she said, then thought about it for a bit. 'He takes me to every shop I want to go to and buys me things, but that's where the excursion ends.'

Would she tell him if she wanted more – a little filmy romance? She grinned and still looking steadfastly at her feet, murmured, 'I cook all kinds of vegetables for him the day he's tired. But sometimes, just to have a little fun, I cook bhindi. I love bhindi and so do my sons, but he hates it and will just get up and leave when he sees the sabzi on his plate! He says, "I'd rather have an apple!"'

I was to understand more about Vishnu's psyche through another couple, altogether, but that wasn't till another day. For now, only this was apparent that he made her happy; that she revelled in cooking the none-too-occasional bhindi to spark a kind of annoyance that is gleefully familiar in a long-term relationship, and that they'd found solidarity as foot-soldiers in a common battle against a common enemy.

As Manju didi and I stood up to leave, Meera insisted on plying us with more chai and having us stay longer, but I promised her I'd be back. She told me she didn't get a lot of visitors, but I reminded her of the bounty of blouses in her closet. That would get customers running to her door, I said and we laughed.

As I walked out, her oldest son made an entrance to help us through the sudden sludge, tearing at the dirt roads outside – we'd just missed a cloudburst (by all appearances, he didn't seem to have caught wind of the stories his mother had told us and that she was guarding from him). Even as I sat down in the car, my companion hissed and pointed to a huddle of men, a few paces from our car. A grey-haired man sat underneath a tree with a few men surrounding him, watching our car with undisguised hostility, 'They're always watching to see who enters and exits her house. They keep wondering if she'll file another complaint.'

The man underneath the tree, she gave me to understand, was the alleged rapist's father.

As we drove off, waving wistful goodbyes to an entire family that stood faithfully in the middle of the road till they'd seen the last of us, I wondered yet again what it was like to be living in that situation. We were leaving Meera behind in that strange ecosystem of conspiratorial silence and hostile men (a man she'd reported for raping her, his family and a coterie of mute spectators). We could steal glances and walk away. Meera had to navigate her peregrinations every day.

Manju didi was quick to assure me of her bravery, though, once I'd brought this up.

'Meera is the leader of our new Rape Survivors' Forum,' she said. 'We started one, a few months ago, to bring together survivors from different states to meet each other and help with the process – psychological, legal, societal; the entire thing.'

I was immensely interested. What did the women talk about when they gathered? But it wasn't just women, Manju didi pointed out, it was men, too – a whole conglomerate of brothers, fathers, husbands and friends, who showed up in solidarity with the survivors.

I was later to meet a man called Kailash, who was on the ad-hoc committee that Meera headed. Kailash's wife had been raped, and the man spent most of his days reaching out to other men, who had wanted to evict their wives for suffering sexual assault. Kailash's story might not find a larger place in the following pages that are dedicated to women, but there have been few men whose words and actions I have been so touched by.

So, Meera, as Manju didi put it, was the then leader of the core ad-hoc committee that convened the Rape Survivors' Forum; it met every couple of months. The forum was organized by various partner-NGOs across states who brought women and men with them to wherever the forum was being held that month – these women and men were usually either in the middle of their legal battle, or just needed a shoulder to cry on, a sympathetic ear that would listen to them and a person who would nod and acquiesce, 'Yes, I went through that, too.'

'Meera is "didi" to so many of those women,' Manju didi proudly told me. 'There is a woman you will meet tomorrow, she'll tell you more about how Meera and her husband helped her and her husband.'

I, of course, asked her how, and Manju didi told me about Ranjini – a survivor I was indeed going to meet the following day – and her husband, Gokul, a Dalit couple who lived in a tiny hamlet populated by dominant-caste Gujjars. She told me about the rape itself, although I had already heard Ranjini's story from her own lips, a month before. But mostly, she told me about what had happened after the rape; about how Gokul mistrusted her with unflinching purpose for a year and a half, keeping his wife at arm's length from him and hurling the most venomous verbal imprecations at her to the tune of 'you were probably never raped'.

It was at Ranjini's lowest, most despairing point that she reached out to her case workers for help and the latter asked Meera if she could find a way to help her heal and perhaps, in the process, find catharsis for her own failed legal battle.

'So, of course she did,' Manju didi said. 'Meera and Vishnu both spoke to Gokul and urged him to see how wrong he was. Thing is, Urmi didi, Vishnu ji is a very nice man but not every partner is. Gokul couldn't handle it. Meera basically said, *"Aapko is waqt apni patni ka saath dena chahiye, aur aap mooh mor rahe ho?* (You should be supporting your wife at this time, and you're turning your back on her?)"'

I heard more about this from Ranjini herself, the next day, but that tiny tidbit about Meera willingly undertaking a venture with an intention to help out with a fellow survivor's relationship, cracked through the veneer of despondency we'd been subsumed by, since the encounter with Meera's nemeses.

If there is one other thing I have taken back from my journey to unearth Meera's story, it is my companion. I had never met Manju before, but to use a phrase she used, two weeks later, over a phone call when I was back in New Delhi and calling to find out how she was, '*kaise achanak se jud gaye the*! (how well we connected, immediately!)'

Manju didi wasn't drawn to this job after a social services degree or an internship or years of employment in peer NGOs. She had never worked before. She grew up, married and continued to live in Dewas, well into her thirties, with her husband and three young sons. She agreed to accompany me to see Meera – upon Ashif's request – eager and compliant, all the while, telling me how she had been Meera's 'case handler' from the beginning, and had kept all her 'notes'. Indeed, Manju didi had an astonishingly exhaustive knowledge of Meera's history, down to the tiniest minutiae, which I had found easy to tap into.

More than anything else, it was evident that she cared.

I'd watched as she grazed the back of Meera's palms when we met her, and asked her all the right questions. I'd watched as her voice automatically softened, without being told to do so, when Meera's son had walked into the room – honed over years of experience with exercising caution. I'd marvelled also at how she let me *be* – a reporter who asked if not probing, then certainly a whole menagerie of curious questions; one after the other, without ever being more than a fly on the wall herself.

That hands-off, quietly respectful camaraderie is possibly what every reporter is desirous of, in a source/handler/fixer. Except, Manju didi was so much more than all of those things, because she cared.

I'd like to record at least one conversation I had with her – our last one before she dropped me at my hotel – because it was after my own heart. Did the job affect her, I asked her, as we reached the hinterland of the city; did she carry what she saw and heard back home with her, wearing it like an invisible cloak of impassivity?

'I used to,' Manju didi told me, simply and gently. 'In the early 2010s, when I first started, I would keep thinking about everything I'd heard through the day – perhaps a survivor I'd met – and carry it home with me. I would snap at my children; withdraw from my husband. I didn't want to do anything "social" that they did. But then I realized, it wasn't just me. Others at the frontline of this work had felt it, too.'

Manju didi had felt oddly comforted by the thought of her discomfort being shared. Ashif, a perceptive boss, had stepped in and hired a counsellor on call to talk to the women and men in his service, whenever they needed to.

'Just one conversation helped me. I didn't talk to her any further,' Manju didi said of her meeting with the mental health practitioner. 'But it was a very good idea. Everyone went to her to ask the same question: how could they stop carrying forward the burden of guilt and pain from what they saw, daily?'

Manju didi is a soft-spoken but feisty social worker, today, who has nerves of steel and her heart in the right place. 'What I love best about this job is its ability to help people. So many of these women you meet, come to trust you more than they do their own families! Where else will you get that? That sort of trust is precious.'

# 3

# Ranjini

## I

I'D NEVER MET RANJINI BEFORE A WISPY, RAIN-DRENCHED Friday morning in July 2018, when I went to her village, but our meeting appeared strangely congruent to the circumstances. The conversation that had begun with Meera and Manju – and had involved Ranjini, without her knowledge – seemed to coalesce seamlessly into the following day, and into our tête-à-tête. When I returned to the circuit house that I'd made my temporary living quarters in Dewas, after interviewing Meera, I felt like some part of me already knew Ranjini. Ranjini leant on Meera, I had learnt. Her husband had not been as stolid and kindly and loving as Vishnu, I had understood. She was receptive to help, I had perceived.

In my mind, I had conjured an image of Ranjini that was based, in equal part on the information that had been relayed by the two women I'd just met, as on telephonic chats with Ranjini, some months hitherto. While investigating (c)old cases for a series on two-finger test survivors, and after a series of conversations with Meera and a few other women, I had arrived at Ranjini through a borrowed telephone number and a circuitous route.

Both Ranjini and her husband, Gokul, had spoken to me, unabashedly and uninhibitedly opening the floodgates to the years of ordeal – sketching the details of her rape, of their conversations with each other's families, of their move to a different village after the rape, and those of their subsequent life together. I was touched at the ease with which they trusted me with their information and I managed to construct a disjointed story out of everything they said on the phone, over a period of several days. Of course, there is a lot which gets left out of a story that is either second-hand or telephonic, and therefore, neither Meera nor Manju in person, nor Ranjini and Gokul over the phone could've conveyed the truest, most comprehensive picture of what had happened.

For instance, who knew that Gokul and Ranjini hadn't spoken to each other for several months after her rape in March 2013 and that she had been miserable and despairing? But then, how could Meera and Manju, who proffered said information, also have prepared me for the utter delight and hellfire-blazing dynamo that Ranjini had been and continues to be?

I'd told them over the phone that I would make the trip to see them soon and sure enough, a few logistical details, a couple of months and a book deal later, I was in Dewas, just a couple hundred kilometres away from them.

Ranjini's case worker called me on the Friday after I'd met Meera. Relatively early in the morning, I walked out my door and into a waiting car with a thirty-something woman called Sangeeta Parmar.

'Have you spoken with Ranjini? What did you think of her?' she got right down to it – one often marvels at how, on reporting tours, as perhaps, on many other excursions far from home, seemingly disparate people are pushed into close quarters and they become fast friends in very little time. Sangeeta and I were embarking on an (at least) three-hour-long car ride to Ranjini's, who lived in a tiny hamlet so far off the beaten track, that I'd been hard-pressed to find it on a state map. We'd have suffered very much in the silence if we hadn't hit it off.

I thought about Sangeeta's question and told her exactly what I remembered – Ranjini had come across as vivacious, exuberant and easy to talk to. She'd opened up to me in a matter of minutes and both she and her husband seemed like amiable people.

'I've been riding out to see her since mid-2013, ever since we first got wind of what had happened in her case,' she said. 'We got to her too late, though. She had already lost in court.'

This was a new one for me. Most social workers who 'handled' proceedings for rape survivors and who

I'd met so far, had navigated the whole route with these women, handholding them through subsequent visits to *thanas* and negotiating the hostile atmosphere of many tiny courtrooms. At what stage could someone step in and still manage to help, post the initial trauma, the hurry and the haste?

I was going to find out. I would find out through observation of the little acts of friendship between these women – a rape survivor and her case worker – who were in no way related, except that they got together that one time, after something terrible had happened. They kept in touch and they talked, and they didn't stop talking even after they'd finished prepping for a court testimony or thumbed through pages of a chargesheet; they swapped stories about their kids and they laughed at anecdotes of their neighbours' antics. They asked after each other's son's performance in class ten, and showed each other reports from a recent doctor's visit to anxiously accrue a 'second opinion' on a mole.

I had rarely seen friendships as real as theirs, develop as a result of something so raw and painful.

## II

THE ROAD TO REACH RANJINI WASN'T EASY. WE STRAYED off the main Indore–Bhopal highway, after having faithfully stuck to it for two hours, and I looked out to see that the cityscape had changed. There were no clusters of settlements anymore. The road of asphalt, too, had ceased to exist; it had given way to loamy, bumpy paths that meandered in every direction. Then, it started raining and finding our way through the thick sheet of rain was rendered impossible – everything looked the same.

Sangeeta had forgotten the way. 'It's been a while,' she said sheepishly, and we stopped to ask at least three groups of cattle-herders before we managed to find it – a lumpen mass of houses that couldn't even be classified a hamlet. We'd left villages far behind. Somewhere inside a house in this cluster, were Ranjini and Gokul.

They found us first.

As our car bumped and ricocheted noisily off the mud path, a smiling couple with bundles of hay on their heads, came running to us. '*Aap hi ho na?* (You're her, aren't you?)' asked a smiling Ranjini and I stupidly acquiesced. Together, Gokul and she led us to their house by walking ahead of our car; that was the first impression of these two people that stayed with me: grinning ear-to-ear, traipsing merrily along the muddy path and showing us the way to their home.

Ranjini's family's reception of the two of us isn't something I'll forget in a hurry – Gokul's mother had canvassed the entire floor of the room with several hollow cement bags, stitched together, to make a seating area for Sangeeta and me, and two young boys (the couple's sons) stared at us curiously from a corner.

Gokul started by telling me how he'd wanted to talk to me on the phone for weeks, but couldn't, '*Yeh phone dekho zara – ispe aapke naam se kisi aur ka number save ho gaya* (If you look at my phone, you'll see – a different number shows up next to your name),' he told me in dismay, brandishing said phone at me, and I corrected the digits for him.

Why did he want to talk to me? I asked. 'We just wanted to chat,' Gokul said affably.

But my eyes were darting swiftly between the earnest Gokul, seated on the empty cement bag before us in perfect lotus pose, and his wife, half-hidden in the shadows behind the door to her room, occasionally smiling in invitation, then springing away.

My travel companion deftly managed to manoeuvre our transition to the one room inside the mud cottage, where Ranjini was now waiting.

The rest of the family stretched out on the large clay porch we'd just been sitting on, staring ahead at one of the most picturesque courtyards I had ever seen, complete with a goat-shed and pots of tulsi plants, bathed in translucent drops from the afternoon rain.

It was an afternoon like no other.

## III

RANJINI DIDN'T MIND PIECING TOGETHER HER STORY for us all over again, for what must've seemed to her like the umpteenth time. What I could tell she *did* mind, was the crack in the door to her room, through which she kept peeping at the shoulders of her husband, evidently wondering if her voice would travel to him.

'You don't have to worry,' I told her gently. 'We'll talk ever-so-softly.' All the same, Sangeeta finally shut the door and we faced one another in a strange kind of darkness; the earthen walls staunchly obfuscating any stray rays of sunshine. The only light in the room was falling poetically on Ranjini's face and on the curly mop of hair on her head, filtered through the canopy of thatch above our heads.

Ranjini had the quality of inspiring complete besottedness. It wasn't just that she was beautiful; her dark skin glowed and accentuated a set of perfectly white, always-set-to-a-grin row of teeth, but she had a fire that blazed deep, dark and low within her.

As we talked, I realized that she also had this quiet, ephemeral quality of immediately making one comfortable – laughing at her own foibles; her eyes dancing in consonance with her mouth. Her voice, which had sounded sing-song to me on the phone, now appeared to complement the rest of her perfectly.

But most of all, it was her gumption that got me.

She was raring full of gumption.

'I didn't know what his intentions were, in the beginning,' she told me quietly, 'neither of us did when we first accepted the offer – it had come to us out of nowhere. This man, far richer than us and of a far more privileged caste, had approached us and said, "I want you to farm my crops for a good fee." It seemed too good to be true.'

It was. Ranjini claimed that she soon realized that his roving eye was part of the package. 'He'd often ask me to stay behind a little longer, tilling an additional part of his grounds, even as my husband made his way home.'

If Ranjini was beginning to suspect that something was off, she could never have guessed that things would come to a head in such a way, a few days before the festival of Holi.

'We'd been farming relentlessly since daybreak. When we finally reached home, it was past six in the evening. I decided to whip up some rotis for dinner, while Gokul cooed to the little one.' Ranjini's youngest daughter was barely four years old at the time.

It was 12 March 2013. Ranjini remembers like it was yesterday, the fact that it had been a Tuesday. 'A day before Holi,' she interjected, 'We couldn't wait to celebrate with the earnings we'd scoured from our work on Balak Ram's fields.' Balak Ram's name was spoken glibly with the suffix of his caste, a clear identifier in Ranjini and Gokul's universe – 'He is a Gujjar,' she said – and Balak Ram Gujjar was, according to her expositions, not a man to be trifled with.

'So, when his man Friday suddenly turned up at the door, an hour after we'd returned from Balak Ram's fields and said, "Saab wants you to come and water the crops," it seemed like he had been sent expecting complete compliance from us. I protested and said that it was too late, but my husband said that we needed the extra cash and followed the man out.'

Within a couple of hours, Ranjini and her little daughter had another visitor – a woman that Ranjini sketchily called Balak Ram Gujjar's 'very close friend'. 'I'm still not sure who she is,' she said in answer to my question, 'just that she seemed like some sort of dependent.'

Anyway, this woman turned up at her doorstep, telling Ranjini that she'd been looking for her and wouldn't she hurry and fetch her shelled and spiced chickpeas because she was in the mood for some?

'I'll tell you now, didi. I don't care much for orders, even if they come from someone higher up in our hierarchy. I flatly refused her and she lost it.'

That woman and Ranjini sparred for a good number of minutes, before the former stalked off. If she'd thought that had concluded her nighttime charades, though, she was mistaken. A few minutes later, she said, Balak Ram himself showed up at the door.

'Why aren't you doing the work that has been assigned to you?' Ranjini remembered Balak Ram asking her with the most immeasurable disdain and fury. 'I'm too tired for any more work,' she said honestly, even as she began to realize that her supplication would do no good. Balak Ram, Ranjini claimed, launched into a vitriolic tirade, hurling the filthiest possible curses at her, even as she gave it back as good as she got.

That was the last straw.

A dam broke. Or somewhere, perhaps – unbeknownst to Ranjini herself – she'd infiltrated the invisible, impenetrable fortress built on ancient yet powerful caste lines. Ranjini had not cowed down; worse still, she had not accepted that she was any smaller than he was. She had believed herself to be his equal.

Balak Ram allegedly rushed towards her with hot white rage.

Ranjini reported struggling with the pile of bedcovers that had, so far, been physically shielding her daughter and her from the verbal wrath of this man. Not anymore. Balak Ram, she alleged, had lunged towards her with a knife, that he'd swooped out from under his vest, and in one fell swoop, sliced her palm.

'I screamed and fell back, but there was no one around. I kept looking around wildly and thinking, *Why did we have to live so far away from everyone else?* Look, even today, these houses are so secluded from the main highway. Before I knew what was happening, he had grabbed my neck in a chokehold, lifted my saree and started raping me.'

'I thought he would stop when he lifted my saree,' Ranjini said quietly, 'I was menstruating. But he didn't. Nothing deterred him. I couldn't muster up enough physical strength to ward him off and his rage had given him some new kind of power.'

'Once he'd finished, I regained my voice and began to threaten to tell on him. "I'll tell everybody," I screamed at him, "I'll make sure you're punished." But he brandished his knife at me again and said, "If you tell anyone, I'll make sure my men abduct you on the road and kill you."'

Ranjini looked steadily at me and continued, '*Main tab bhi nahi darri, didi.* (I still wasn't scared.)' But at this point, my husband entered the picture. It was about

10 in the night and he'd been walking homewards, when he heard my screams from a distance. He began to run towards our house.'

According to Ranjini, Balak Ram met him at the door, bloodied knife still clutched in his fist. 'Get away from here or I'll stab you,' Gokul's employer reportedly yelled at him, but Gokul didn't budge. The duo wrestled, Ranjini claimed, even as Balak Ram began to pant and taunt him at the same time, 'What can a lowly Korku like you, do to me?' Almost on the heels of this taunt – as if spurred by its poisonous jab – Balak Ram threw Gokul to the ground, his fall broken by the dirty stream of the *nala* that he landed in, back first.

It had only been ten minutes past ten. Balak Ram, Ranjini claimed, then disappeared into the darkness.

The husband and wife exchanged almost no words, 'He knew,' she said simply and walked, instead, to where the rest of the family stayed, to tell them the story of what had happened. Ranjini's two older children – her sons – were, incidentally, away at a friend's, that night.

The family debated through the night, among themselves, and postponed the visit to the thana to the morning. Why didn't they go immediately? 'They wanted me to rest,' she said, with the ominous resignation of someone who had clearly weathered more battles on that front, between that night and the time of her telling of this story.

Ranjini's family was never truly convinced.

# IV

A MOTLEY GROUP OF THREE MADE IT TO THE LOCAL police station the next morning, Ranjini – Gokul and his father. But if she was looking for succour here, she was about to be disappointed.

'We went straight to the sub-inspector on duty and told him what had happened. He listened and once he was done listening, asked us to wait and ignored us pointedly for the rest of the time. We sat on a wooden bench near the entryway and waited ... and waited. We were there for hours, hungry and thirsty, afraid to leave, in case we were called in suddenly, and yet, there was no summoning.'

Ranjini recalled the number of times she made it to the front desk and pleaded her case. 'It was no use,' she smiled sadly, 'a couple of Balak Ram's relatives were *thaanedar*s and they'd clearly heard the news. They just looked at me and smirked.'

The cops finally summoned her at 5 p.m., she told me. 'They asked me the most abhorrent questions,' she protested vociferously. 'It was as if they'd been waiting since the morning for such an opportunity. One of them said, "So you were raped, huh? How do you know you were raped? Do you know what rape is?" Another jeered at me and asked, "Did he make you lie down or were you sitting up?" and everybody laughed.'

Ranjini reiterated, '*Main tab bhi nahi darri*. My husband was called in, a few minutes later, and he was asked ridiculous questions, too, like, "What is your religion? Which god do you pray to?" He lost his calm and screamed, "How does it matter? Does my caste or religion obstruct me from getting justice here?"'

Ranjini didn't lose her gumption that day, she told me; instead, she began to gesticulate wildly for the whole station to take notice and demanded that her FIR be filed immediately if these men didn't want her heading to Dewas to report them to their superiors. 'They were flustered and one of them said rather suggestively, "If you register this complaint, we cannot guarantee that such a thing won't happen to you again."'

But the couple would have none of it. An FIR was reluctantly registered.

It didn't end there. Time had rolled on and it was late evening by the time Ranjini (with her husband and father-in-law in tow) was sent to the government district hospital for her medical examination. '*Par humare pehle toh call pahuch jaati hai* (Unfortunately, the phone call against us arrives before we do),' she smiled resignedly.

Sangeeta chimed in, 'In most cases of an assault by someone "higher up", you can safely assume that he has his cronies to pinch-hit for him, even in his absence.' These pinch-hitters, she suggested, could be found in the guise of police lackeys and hospital employees, who make proceedings that much harder for a survivor of a disadvantaged caste.

Ranjini was about to battle a few of Balak Ram's lackeys at the hospital, who were deputed, she believed, to further delay legal proceedings.

'Those men – his friends from the village – weren't letting us in at first,' she said in disbelief, 'They said we were too late. But we knew our rights and shouted our way in. After that, they pretty much left us alone. Balak Ram's paternal cousin was an attendant there, so I knew this would happen. I went up to an attendant myself and asked if she could, at least, give me some ointment for the cut in my hand where Balak Ram's knife had gashed it. She looked at it coldly and said, "*Kahan lagi hai?* (Where is the bruise?)" and walked off.'

A second female attendant finally arrived to escort Ranjini into an examination room. And it was here that Ranjini's case mirrored Meera's, down to the most despicable minutiae – she was made to undergo the two-finger test. I knew this because Ashif, back in his office, Kranti, on the phone, and Sangeeta, during the car ride to Ranjini's, had told me as much, multiple times. I knew that her case had been filed, like scores others like her, under the 'two-finger' nomenclature of rape survivor histories; cases that set apart the bad from the worst; cases that could be codified as the most abhorrent in medical negligence.

But if I had read her case file through the cold, staccato words of bureaucracy – words like 'hymen', 'laxity', 'virginity', 'a Supreme Court ban' float up in my memory – the words faded away in front of Ranjini's very real, raw and guttural ones, 'She inserted the whole of her two fingers inside me.'

There was silence once she'd said this, as we considered the purport of the words, of the immense medico-legal-feministic perspectives one could tear them down with. '*Kya aapko pata tha ki yeh galat hai?* (Did you know what she did was wrong?)' I asked.

Ranjini shook her head and bobbed her head once at Sangeeta. 'Didi told me, weeks later, after I'd met with the officials of Jan Sahas, that this wasn't usually done. But at the time, I just wanted my "medical" done.'

The 'medical', Ranjini claimed, was a harrowing experience even without the inclusion of the two-finger test. Once her doctor had finished the first leg of her exam – inserting two fingers inside Ranjini's vagina to confirm tightness, as opposed to 'laxity' – she allegedly looked at her and said to her face, 'Have you really been raped?'

Ranjini's MLC, which I have pored over, makes mention of the fact that 'her vagina easily admits two fingers'. It also casually and ridiculously states, 'Lady is used to sexual intercourse and she is mother of three children (sic) so we cannot say rape.'

Once again, it didn't end there. 'When she saw that I'd been menstruating, she immediately became suspicious of everything I had been saying,' continued Ranjini. 'She said, "How can he have raped you while you're in this condition? Surely *this* would have deterred him." I thought that was funny, didi. Because I had thought the same thing when he'd lifted my saree. But it hadn't stopped him.'

Her examining doctor's 'suspicions' were apparently also compounded when Ranjini filled 'Korku' in the space next to 'Caste' on her medical form. '"Why would he touch a Dalit like you?" she said to me in surprise.'

The many ways in which Ranjini's medical examination is a blot on the treatment rape survivors receive at hospitals, can also be found in the details of Meera's case. I have already outlined what the guidelines state, how hospitals rampantly conducted the test before the Supreme Court ban (it was incidentally ordered in May 2013, just two months after Ranjini's two-finger test), and how a menstruating woman should be examined a second time for certainty, among other requirements. Yet, even if one were to disregard all other factors, shouldn't the most intrinsic human sensitivity have played a role here?

# V

AFTER THAT ORDEAL, RANJINI, GOKUL AND HER FATHER-in-law returned home. Their return solicited a beginning. The beginning to a wait so long and so arduous that most people would've given up. The ability to haul your battered psyche to a courtroom where you're subjected to the most insidious forms of mistrust, is already a hard enough thing to do. For Ranjini, though? The battle was harder at home.

'My husband stopped talking to me completely.' Her voice had lowered to the husk of a shell, barely ricocheting off the ends of her *pallu* that she was now staring down into.

I realized that this was the moment she'd been unsure about, speaking about her husband's injustices, sitting merely metres from him and his family.

But Sangeeta had shut the door, firmly edging a stray log of wood into an inch of free space beneath it, and conversation was resumed.

'He didn't talk to me for almost two years. And it was all because of what he heard in that courtroom.'

Ranjini's court struggles had begun as sketchily as her run-ins with the police. For a month after the recording of her testimony, she withdrew into herself. She talked about how she shunned strangers, so much so that when a team from the NGO came to visit her, she refused to meet them, 'I thought it was Balak Ram's accomplices. His goons were threatening us every day,' and Jan Sahas couldn't gain access to her until some months into her court hearings.

'I was worried he would try to sneak in a *raazinama* through someone, that I might unwittingly sign. So when Jan Sahas would turn up with sheaves of paper to get me acquainted with my own case and the injustices that I could fight, I wouldn't look at them or read them.'

Her trust was ultimately won, but not before she was on her way to losing her case.

'It was inevitable, didi,' said Ranjini. 'There were no witnesses. And when Balak Ram's defence lawyer called a lady cop to the stand, she began to talk about how I had taken ₹40,000 from the accused and had now turned my back on him to fleece him for more money. I lost it!'

Ranjini recalled charging at her even as the latter did the same, the pair meeting mid-scuffle in the courtroom,

'They had to separate us, there was so much *hungama*', and the room descended into an uneasy quiet.

However, that was the last straw for her husband's already chary mind. Gokul, Ranjini admitted, had been 'completely turned' at this new 'information' about a ₹40,000-deal.

'I don't know if he was already thinking it, but now, it was all I heard every day: "You took *chaalis hazaar rupaiya* from him. You must have known that he was coming that night. How could you not have known? Perhaps you loved him? Surely you spoke to him when we used to be in his fields." There was no end to his rambling.'

It wasn't the rambling of a petulant child; it was the cruel vituperation of a husband she had expected, at the least, to receive love and support from. In fact, his became the shared consciousness of the whole family. Gokul's parents – who had welcomed the duo and their children into their midst after the rape ('We just couldn't keep living in that accursed house anymore') – seemed to share their son's sentiments and blew hot and cold with Ranjini, if only in slightly muted ways than her husband.

I looked straight into Ranjini's face. Behind the bird-like, sparkling, kohl-lined eyes was deep pain: 'Did you never reprimand him for his behaviour?' I demanded, indignant on her behalf. 'I did!' she smiled, becoming again the same Ranjini I was just beginning to know and admire. 'In fact, one day, frustrated with his monosyllabic responses, I told him I was going to leave him and that he could very well take care of the kids on his own. But when I asked the kids who they'd rather stay with, they said, "*Humein mummy bhi chahiye, papa bhi chahiye* (We want both, our mum and our dad)." Well, that did it.'

Ranjini laughed as she said, 'It reminded me of a movie I had once seen. I don't know why I thought of it at that exact moment. I can't remember what it's called but it had a lovely song. What kind of film? Something with the husband and wife splitting up but becoming confused about what to do with their kids.'

'Any time he brought up the money issue, too, I had a ready answer for him, "If I had taken the ₹40,000, don't you think you would've seen some shiny new things around the house? Have you seen me buy anything? *Sab kuch toh hum saath mein hi khareedte hai.* (We buy everything together.)" I thought he softened a little after that.'

Gokul came around for good, however, through the most bizarre incident I had ever heard anyone narrate. 'Balak Ram came to our village one day, I'm not sure why. I think he was just cocksure and wanted to do a little victory jig, and I was incensed that he thought he could do that while *my* family thought I should hide my face. I just saw red. I don't know what came over me but suddenly, in a mad rage, I turned to my husband and said, "Today you'll know the truth." I rushed to the tubewell near our house, where I could see a pair of someone's muddy, soiled slippers. I picked up a slipper and ran after that man. I just rained down on him with that *chappal*, beating him black and blue. I didn't stop. Balak Ram was so astonished he didn't know what to do. He just looked at me as I hit him, and I near ran him out of our village, screaming "You said I took money? *I* took money?" Whenever anyone tried to come close to help him, I just shouted some more, "*Koi beech mein nahi aayega* (No one must come any closer)." That was it. He left our village, bruised from my beating, and hasn't come back since.'

I stared at her for a full minute, agape, as she smiled.

'So, after that? Gokul believed you?'

'Yes, when I returned to the house, he said simply, "*Ab mujhe yakeen hai ki tumne paise nahi liye* (Now I believe that you didn't take any money.)"'

The exposition was dissatisfactory to me, 'But was that it? He didn't apologize? You didn't want to ask him why he hadn't believed you all these months?'

'Nahi, didi,' said Ranjini. 'I just wanted that chapter closed.'

I asked her how she felt, right after having chased out her alleged assailant.

'Strong,' she remembered. 'I could feel the power in my arms when I hit him. It was like I was finally hitting him back for everything he'd done to me. It was also strange, because all that time, as I saw him cowering underneath my blows, I could remember how I'd felt when he was raping me: powerless. I had thought, until that point, that I was not very strong. But I proved myself wrong.'

I imagined a 'powerless' Ranjini wielding a new-fangled power to reclaim her own body, her spirit, her soul. It was not hard to imagine.

# VI

AT SOME POINT DURING THE CONVERSATION, WE WERE interrupted by a high, shrill voice from the courtyard and Ranjini's voice broke into a smile. 'That's my little one,' she said, and sure enough, the creaking door that had caused an adjunct between Ranjini's whispers and her husband's family outside, was thrown open to let in a diminutive, curly-haired girl in a bright salwar kameez.

This, I understood was her youngest child, her eight-year-old daughter who had been a toddler at the time when Balak Ram had allegedly entered their home, uninvited. This was the baby Ranjini claimed she had sought to protect that night.

Piu skipped about, near her mother, as the latter urged her to scoop up her lunch into a plate from a large clay pot outside. 'She comes home from school for a mid-break lunch,' her mother explained. 'She gets about an hour.'

I watched as Ranjini busied herself for a couple of minutes, stroking back her daughter's curls fondly, curls which resembled her own, and ladled out hot dal on a steel plate. As Piu raced off to a corner of the courtyard to eat her lunch, next to a calf tethered there, I asked Ranjini how she and Gokul had met.

'My parents arranged it,' she said, without a hint of shyness. 'One day, they said a young man was coming to see me, and I got to talk to him in private for two minutes. He told me, "Look, I'm very dark because I work in the fields all day. Will that be a problem?" I told him, "Your complexion's dark, but I hope your heart isn't. That's all that matters!"'

After that, the duo was married off quickly and Ranjini moved two and a half hours away from her parents'. 'But I still visit home quite often. My mother isn't alive anymore, but my father and an older brother are and they live in our old house. In fact, I just went up to see them on Thursday.'

~

Ranjini's carefree childhood was an easy one to read on her independent shoulders, the head she held high, the quick-witted retorts she hurled at people with dissident opinions. That childhood was also writ large on her right forearm, where, interestingly, she had a large black tattoo of her name, circled by an 'Om'. She said she'd got it done at a winter fair that her parents had taken her to.

Did she love her husband? It wasn't hard to fathom, even though it was somewhere behind the toothy grins and the unruffled exterior. At one point, when I told her how much I loved her curls, she tossed them back and laughed, '*Hain na bilkul mere pati jaise?* (Aren't they exactly like my husband's?)' Until she'd pointed it out, I hadn't noticed the similar ringlets that dotted Gokul's forehead.

Ranjini spoke to me of the little land she 'owned'. 'It's about one and a half acres, *shayad do bigha*, of land that belongs to the forestry department,' she said sheepishly.

'After we moved here, into my husband's parents' house, we were still not entirely comfortable. I was always afraid that he would be back and besides, the villagers were always staring. So we moved away to a little lump of land we discovered in the middle of nowhere, built our cottage and fielded the land there.'

'Where was this exactly?' Ranjini raised a thin, long finger in one direction, but as far as the flecks of her nail would point – and try as I might have, to look into the distance through a heavy sheet of perpendicular rain – I could see nothing.

'It's actually not very far,' piped up her daughter, who'd come back to this homely, indolent scene, having finished her lunch. 'I could take you!'

I wholeheartedly agreed, but first, her mother insisted, Sangeeta and I must have some chai. And here it was again – a friendship-fostering mug of steamy, too-sugary goodness that had been offered to me across the length and breadth of my trips, somehow always around the time that new confidences had been forged.

I've never forgotten that afternoon. I'm not sure why. I remember distinct shapes, sounds and smells from that witch hour and I can almost view myself as though from an external vantage point – sitting akimbo on a doorstep in Ranjini's house, looking wistfully into rain-splattered green fields through a hole in a stack of hay.

I can remember the tiny weight of Ranjini's daughter, leaning against me on the not-so-wide frame of that doorstep that we were both sharing, our feet almost touching. I can remember the little girl pointing at my anklets in wonder and then nudging me towards her mother's far thicker set of ankle ornaments as I found myself saying that those were more beautiful. I can remember the scent of sugar mixed in three spoonfuls of tea, swirling in a pan of hot milk – a smell that mingled with the scent of earth, cow dung, mould and other smells I had never smelled before, in conjunction. I remember that I looked this way and that, smiled at everyone around me and watched as they smiled back in slight puzzlement, even as I did the most puzzling thing of all: fight the tenacious urge to cry.

To date, I have never been able to fathom exactly why I had wanted to cry then, but I suspect that something about the being-so-close-to-nature and smelling odours and thinking inexplicable things that I've never since been able to recall, brought me to tears. There was something bewitching and beguiling about the afternoon, a silence that wasn't rent asunder by the distant sound of cow-bells or rain on cakes of dung.

Ranjini's daughter, Piu, broke my reverie when she began a conversation with Sangeeta in earnest, about her school uniform. 'They'll be handing them out next week,' she explained. 'I've already been fitted for mine, a white shirt and a purple skirt. Till then, we can wear whatever we want,' she said, pointing to her salwar kameez by way of explanation.

I told her that my uniform used to be white and maroon, and tried to point to a square of colour on my kurta to show a close resemblance. I drank my tea. I watched as Sangeeta received phone call after phone call; I was vaguely surprised at the network reception. I listened with interest as my Dewas collaborator explained that she had been drafted into her non-profit's 'helpline service', which meant she had to take calls from survivors or their families at any odd time of the day or night, talking them out of (often suicidal) despair and reassuring them of justice.

Within minutes, our motley crew was ready to depart to see Ranjini's mystery cottage – Sangeeta and I, Ranjini, her husband and their three children, Piu and two older sons, who had just joined us.

We started to walk across a tiny path, only somewhat visible between human-sized stalks of grass to both, our left and right. We allowed our feet to make squelching sounds as we traipsed through mud and 'watched out' for puddles that 'might have reptiles,' Ranjini informed us – the very picture of bucolic utopia. We soon reached.

Ranjini's mystery house was worth it. I hardly believe words will paint a deserving picture, but I shall attempt to draw a textual postcard for the reader. There were undulating slopes of green grass in front of us (must be 'do bigha', I assumed, since everyone had been saying so), and in the middle of the green slopes, like a mirage, shone a sparkly, shimmery blue pond. 'We dug the pond ourselves,' Ranjini's eldest said with pride. I walked to the edge of that pond and looked in. I had never seen cleaner blue in a waterway 'created' by human hands. When I looked back, I saw the house itself – a thatched cottage with an adjoining shed for cows.

It was picturesque.

Two dogs barked in the distance. 'One of them is Julie, and the other, Tipu,' said my brave Ranjini. 'I got them after the ... They never leave my side. Whenever a stranger wanders around here, they bark loudly and scare them away. I feel less on edge with them around.'

The dogs, as though on cue, bounded up to her waiting hands.

Why the choice of habitat which was this far away from their old home? Gokul said they'd fallen in love with the land – the green 'slopes' obscured them from view, while Ranjini admitted she'd wanted to take up the project of doing up lands which were barren when they moved in. Once again, she stressed how these lands weren't theirs for the keeping, but the forestry department's: 'Even a couple of officials came, once, asking about them and scolding us.'

'What did they say? What did you do?' I asked her.

'I told them, "You people have neglected this land for so long. You wouldn't even know it existed if we hadn't started cultivating it." I told them that we would take care of the land on their behalf, grow many, many plants and certainly share our produce thereafter. After all, wouldn't they like labour they didn't have to pay for?' Ranjini quipped with the usual twinkle in her eye, and I assumed, safely, that she'd won her argument.

Her eldest told me he'd even made a video at the time. 'I didn't think they were going to leave us alone so easily. In fact, a few times, some people claiming to be from the department did come, ordering us out. But I made this video, showcasing all the great work my mother and father had done, and displaying all the greenery. I, then, put it up on Facebook. They never came back.'

I have watched that video and I could tell you that few things mirror the earnestness of a video clip made to save a home and a homemade pond.

Sangeeta and I sat with the family for a while, on the now-familiar earthen floor of their cottage and we watched the rain for a bit, as Ranjini talked about her case some more. 'When I got into it at first, I had not been prepped by Jan Sahas. So I hardly knew what to say in court. But now, this second time around, I've been taught well and I'll hold my ground. I won't lose the appeal,' she said in steely determination.

Her conviction of the truth and her alleged assailant's guilt hasn't dimmed in all these years.

I had wondered throughout this trip, and on many trips before and after, about how many survivors could continue to pick up the fight, even after they'd seemingly lost their case. I found my answer in Ranjini's way of life – she lived like she had already won, because *she* believed she was telling the truth, whether a court convicted the man she'd accused or not.

That kind of living had set her free.

The last time I saw Ranjini's family was when our car rounded a corner over the rained-down, undulating village road. I looked back to see five figures, resplendent in the rain, and five hands waving vigorously.

## VII

IN THE PAST COUPLE OF YEARS, RANJINI AND I HAVE spoken often. In terms of her case, she has had nothing new to tell me at any of those times. True to form, though, she is never fazed by the questions – displaying, instead, a vehemence that lent itself to the notion of the crime having been committed – and her case reaching court, yesterday.

Little changes have emerged.

Piu graduated her fourth standard with good marks.

Her eldest son didn't fare excellently at his twelfth standard board exams and caused Ranjini quite a bit of worry about where he'd get admission. We spent a few minutes, every few weeks after the dates of the results, dissecting how best to ensure his college dream wasn't cut short – me offering to Google forms and dates and the ilk; Ranjini wanting to take the bus to Dewas to physically source them. One day, however, she called excitedly to tell me that her son was making the move to the city – to Indore – for college. Ranjini sounded proud, her decibel having risen a few tiny notches. A few months later, in April 2020, she mentioned going to visit him often, with Gokul. 'He doesn't come home nearly as much,' she laughed.

Little changes, then.

In terms of the legal machinery, however – and the peregrinations of her life's events around caste – she is exactly where she started. At a stalemate.

April 2020. A hot five o'clock on a Friday evening.
*Swoosh.*
*Swoosh.*
The sound of a scythe lacerating the thick evening air,
repeated rhythmically in the background as with each
fell swoop, Ranjini hacked at stalks of *gehu* (wheat).
One golden-hued stalk after another. *Swoosh. Swoosh.*
She sliced each into thinner fragments to grind into flour,
she explained, to later mould into hot chapatis.

It was a pleasant opening to a phone call, her
*swooshing* and *swishing* pulsing in time with the sound
of her occasional laughter.

We spoke of her son's college escapades before we
reached the inevitable question of the appeal. Post her
failing to get a conviction in the district court and filing
an appeal in Madhya Pradesh High Court, Ranjini had
heard nothing – no summons in more than three years.

Did she still think about the rape?

'Every day,' she responded.

'I am still fearful,' she said, uncharacteristically
betraying a crack in her steely veneer. 'Everyone knows
where we live and no one's on our side. What if they
were to gang up with him and finish us off?'

Why would they do that? 'They never stood up for
me then. Most of the families in these parts are either
of his caste or want to suck up to him because he does
them favours or gives them odd jobs on his land. Even
in 2013, right after I had filed my FIR, most of them
would harangue me, "Why are you complaining against

him? He's a powerful man. Why would he attack you?"
Later, when I lost my case, they said, "We knew you
were making it up all along. Wouldn't he have been
found guilty, otherwise?"'

Eerily like in Meera's case, Ranjini spoke bitterly of
how no witnesses testified for her in court. 'They knew
what had happened. A couple of houses are also very
close to ours. How could they not have heard?'

In juxtaposition to her account of how her husband
had overheard her screams from a distance, I understood
her incredulity.

The house in the middle of nowhere and the two dogs
were also suddenly beginning to make more sense.

'Every time I see him – even from a distance –
roaming about, I think, "why isn't he in jail?" I'll worry
for as long as he walks free.'

In the most straightforward and linear calculation of
time, it's been seven years since Ranjini was raped.

In many ways, it's been no time at all.

# 4

# Caste and Sexual Assault

BETWEEN TEN YEARS, FROM 2007 TO 2017, THERE HAS been a 66 per cent growth in crimes against Dalits in India.

The rape of Dalit women, National Crime Records Bureau (NCRB) data shows, has doubled in those ten years. The NCRB, incidentally, was established in 1986 'to function as a repository of information on crime and criminals so as to assist the investigators in linking crime to the perpetrators'.[1]

In 2015, the NCRB found that the number of (registered) rapes against Dalit women had gone up from 1,346 in 2009 to 2,233 in 2014.[2]

The same data (collated in 2015) also found that six Dalit women are raped in India every day. This is in stark contrast to figures from 2006, where data claimed that nearly three Dalit women were raped on a daily basis, projecting an obvious doubling of the numbers in this period. And if this wasn't sobering enough, the most recent compilation from the NCRB's stables – its crime record, published in 2020 – found that on an average, ten Dalit women were raped daily, last year.³ From 2006 to 2015 and on to 2020, therefore, we've only seen an alarming rise in the numbers, from three to six to ten. Ten women, across twenty-eight states. Ten women, wherever they are. Ten women, who identify as Dalit, have their bodies taken at will. Every day.

It is important to note that this data says nothing of the large number of crimes that go unreported, variously because of social shame, familial pressures and the collusion between the nexus of dominant-caste perpetrators and local police officials in quashing a case.

A 2014 report published by Amnesty International quoted Divya Iyer, Senior Researcher at the organization's India wing, as saying, 'Members of dominant castes are known to use sexual violence against Dalit women and girls as a political tool for punishment, humiliation and assertion of power.'⁴

The same report also asserted, 'Crimes against Dalits are often not properly registered or investigated, conviction rates are low, and there is a large backlog of cases. Police are also known to collude with perpetrators from dominant castes in covering up crimes, by not registering or investigating offences against Dalits.'⁵ Aren't Meera and Ranjini glaring examples of the nexus between cops, panchayats and dominant-caste perpetrators of rape? In the cases of both Dalit women, their Dalit status was used as an apparatus to silence them at every step of the way to getting justice. While both women filled out their caste on a medical form that had nothing to do with the actual atrocities they had faced, they also fought an uphill battle to get there; one that would deter the most stoic of spirits.

The fact that they were raped *because* they were Dalit, is undeniable. The fact that their caste identities – which situated them right at the bottom of the Hindu caste pool – marked them for rape, is indisputable. The fact that their social identifiers made them easy pickings for political domination, today, stares India right in its privileged-caste face.

Why was Meera raped? Rape is about power, yes, but in her case, it was also about one-upmanship; about a dominant-caste man attempting to show a less-than-privileged caste family – or rather, man, his inability to 'protect' his woman. At the heart of her rape, also, was the quintessential and sordid conflict over land – in Meera's case, localized by the geographies of a boundary wall – playing itself out through the subordination of a woman's body. Meera had to 'pay the price' for daring to share a wall with a man 'higher up' than she was; she had to be penalized for venturing into his 'pure, dominant-caste' environs without bowing her head, keeping an arm's distance from him, considering herself his inferior or even lowering her voice when she spoke to him. Indeed, even as an entire family rebelled against a very archaic delineation of land, laid down by a caste system that privileged others at the cost of their oppression, it was she who became the marked woman who needed to be taught a lesson. Her rape, and that of Ranjini's are both startling and horrifying, in that they are recorded to have been committed in rage. A rage of disbelief at their defiance as Dalits.

Ranjini was raped, allegedly by her employer, who was rendered even more powerful by the feudal set-up they lived in. She refused to comply when he called her, and through that single act, seemed to have 'sealed her fate'. In Ranjini's graphic description of the violence committed against her, the fact that she was menstruating did not deter her rapist and yet, it was a fact that was brought up, ever so callously, by a lackadaisical medical team which reportedly scoffed at the fact that someone would rape her *even after* knowing that she was Dalit and on her period – the double whammy of 'impurity'.

Both women had to face the brunt of a reluctance on the part of local cops to even register their FIRs. Both report having to sit in thanas for hours, injured and bleeding, waiting for someone to pay attention to them. Both, importantly, allege the inevitability of there being 'someone who knew their perpetrator' at the police station, the government hospital, or among the goons who would reportedly have been set on them.

They report, also, the reluctance of entire villages to get involved.

The seismic attempt to silence their voices, at both a societal/*gram* level and an executive/policing level, has continued unabated over the years. If either Meera or Ranjini would have chosen to give up, no one would have batted an eyelid – it would have been a tiny blip on the largely impenetrable waters of the Hindu caste pool.

The systemic violence perpetrated against them and the gaslighting of their testimonies will, perhaps, best be remembered in 2020 – an unnatural year – by an unnatural manifestation of cruelty: when the life of a nineteen-year-old Dalit woman from Hathras, Uttar Pradesh,[6] was packed away in a plume of smoke – she was burnt after she was raped, as dissidents argued against the upper-caste-ness of her rapists with privileged impunity of her rapists. Hauled away by the scruff of her dupatta (did you say salwar kameezes deter rape?) and raped by four men in a field she knew, she spent two weeks dying in a hospital, yet supplying every detail of her rape, only to be hauled away again – this time, in death – to a cremation pyre made ready for her, an inconvenient survivor, burnt down a convenient way.

The systemic violence in this case is reminiscent of the Dalit girl from April 2018, who was allegedly raped for several months by three dominant-caste men, before she landed up at the Satna police station in Madhya Pradesh, to file a report with a six-month-old foetus wrapped in a plastic bag.[7]

The systemic violence is reminiscent of the gang rape and murder of two teenage Dalit girls in Badaun, Uttar Pradesh in 2014, by the dominant-caste people of their community, when they left home in the still of the night to relieve themselves.[8] You probably remember the image of two lifeless female forms with their necks broken, bodies crumpled, dangling precariously off a tree branch, printed, that year, on several front pages and, more recently, on a Bollywood film poster with Ayushmann Khurrana as the lead.

Systemic violence is reminiscent of the strange and horrific kangaroo court justice of 2015, when an unelected khap panchayat* ordered the rape of two Dalit sisters as 'punishment' or revenge for their brother eloping with a dominant-caste woman from their village in Baghpat, Uttar Pradesh, in northern India.[9]

You could possibly trace the systemic violence – in graphic circles and loops all around cities and towns and villages, and across the decades past – to the Bhotmanges of Kherlanji and Bant Singh of Punjab; countless recorded instances of Dalit women stripped naked and paraded before being gang raped, all in an unremitting order of 'punishment'.

Who does this punishment appease? Clearly, the harbingers and upholders of a fragile caste order, desperate to secure its sanctity against all challengers, but mostly, women.

'The levels of oppression are multiple,' says Ashif Shaikh, whose organization, Jan Sahas, notes innumerable cases of atrocities against Dalit women, weekly. 'One of the biggest problems is that of counter-cases. This means that when a Dalit woman or her family tries to file an FIR against someone for rape, the latter usually finds

---

* A khap is a community organization representing a clan or a group of related clans. A khap panchayat is an assembly of khap elders.

a way to file a counter-case against them, confident that it'll stick. Often, these are cases of land disputes or allegations that the family owes them money. For instance, in the case of Meera, after she filed her FIR with such difficulty, her husband was beaten up and the perpetrator also claimed that she and her husband were encroaching on his land. This is to provoke the survivor to come to a "compromise". The strategy is usually successful.'

Shaikh echoes the idea of a violence that is perpetuated in order to 'teach someone a lesson'. 'Perpetrators, in such cases, often prey on the idea of "shame". Sometimes, the rape is a result of land-based violence and the woman's body becomes the means to shame the family into thinking, "*Mere saath bahut galat hua hai* (I have been severely wronged)", so that they'll inevitably leave. Sometimes, it's rage at the power women from oppressed sections seem to be acquiring in front of their eyes; for instance, when they watch a Dalit woman go out to get a job, or travel to college for her studies.'

Shaikh can't stress enough that what has changed is the easy readiness – the contumaciousness of these women to keep fighting, sometimes for years on end.

In early 2019, I reported on a case of how a mother and her minor daughter have been caught up in a battle against rape for years, in a tiny hamlet in Jhansi, Uttar Pradesh.[10] The daughter had been allegedly stalked for years, before being raped by a group of dominant caste Thakur men. Time and again, she came up against intransigent police officials who, at one point, even delayed going to their help when the mother and daughter phoned to complain of public harassment – reportedly, because they'd been warned against it by the men.

The irony in this case was that the mother had finally decided to voice their combined struggles at a national platform and had participated in a 'Dignity March' or 'Garima Yatra', organized by groups of civil society members. This march, meant to highlight what they were going through at home, was led by rape survivors – mostly Dalits and their friends and family members – and featured colourful stopovers at various spots across the length and breadth of the country, that the women were traversing on foot. The Garima Yatra went on between January–March 2019, for a period of sixty days; and for many of these women, this was the first time that they were stating the truth to a power that held them captive at home.

Funny that while the mother took solace in the applause and the camaraderie that the faceless cities offered, she understood far too quickly upon her return, that it had caused a suspicious community back home, to harangue and plague her daughter for precisely that crusade what the mother had been doing outside the village.

A false reality had warped the woman when she left the more obvious caste shackles at home, but what about when she returned to its microcosm, where most of her city audiences didn't follow? At the time of my interview with her, she and her husband had just escaped a mob of irate men and women, who had heckled them in the middle of the village *chowrasta* for maligning the village name before outsiders. 'Please, *kuch kijiye*,' she sobbed helplessly over multiple phone calls, amidst the formulation of terrified and half-baked plans to move out of the village, if and when she was able to save up the money.

She was inevitably rescued by policemen, who had been rushed to the spot by calls from supervisors after Jan Sahas had phoned in. The mother had told me that when first attempting to file an FIR in her daughter's case, the district police had told her, 'Why don't you settle it with the khap panchayat?' So she had tried and the men of the khap, she said, had merely asked the accused to apologize to her daughter and urged the family not to wash their dirty linen in public again.

In November 2017, a Human Rights Watch report found that sexual violence survivors often face humiliation at police stations and hospitals, noting that, 'In several cases, the police resisted filing the FIR or pressured the victim's family to "settle" or "compromise", *particularly if the accused was from a powerful family or community*' (emphasis added).[11] This is precisely what happened with the mother and daughter in this case.

Lamenting the absence of a witness protection law in India that could help in the eventuality of such forced 'compromises', the HRW report also noted that 'Khap Panchayats, unofficial village caste councils, often pressure Dalit and other so-called "low-caste" families not to pursue a criminal case or to change their testimony if the accused is from the dominant caste.'[12]

None of the women I reported on, for this book, succumbed to this pressure. But it is undeniable that the odds are stacked outrageously against them. If Meera or Ranjini or that brave mother-daughter duo had, in fact, chosen to give in to the compromises which the HRW analysis finds most women in their position are forced to make, no one would have batted an eyelid.

Let that sink in.

I still don't know if Meera or Ranjini will win in a court of law. But their defiance, stretched out over incalculable swathes of time, has already flouted the rigidity of a caste system no one said they could win against.

Yet, perhaps, they still might.

# 5

# Pia

## I

I CAN REMEMBER VIVIDLY WHEN I FIRST HEARD OF PIA. In the middle of making a documentary on Nidhi – approximately two years since her rape – to accentuate her journey, I was asked by the editors at my workplace if I wanted to explore the story of 'that little baby ... have you seen ... very similar to this one.' I knew of the baby they were referring to; I'd followed the bulletins on her case almost daily since it had happened: her rape and the arrest of her twenty-eight-year-old cousin, the alleged perpetrator.

That baby was rapidly becoming the nation's darling and the epitome – the very embodiment of the collective conscience of a nation that had failed – over and over again – to thwart rape. Pia's story had emerged out of her nondescript northwest Delhi shanty and had evoked outrage across the length and breadth of the country. She had found herself making headlines here and abroad, and suddenly, miraculously, becoming the subject of Supreme Court debates and governmental interventions.

But in terms of her story, I'm getting ahead of myself.

I would like to tell Pia's story the way I learned it, piecing it together through my many meetings with her family. It was long after the stories had been written and filed, then filed away, far from the peregrinations of the news cycle, that a friendship began to bloom between the family and me, which exists to this day.

So it happened that somewhere right after Nidhi's documentary had been shot, edited and digitally released, Pia's story found me. I had wanted to know more. I was driven by the urge to investigate, in fact, if there was any prospect of our media outlet to do for the eight-month-old rape survivor, what it had done for Nidhi – raising money through a crowdfunding campaign.

The rape had occurred on the morning of a Sunday, on 28 January 2018. At the point that I set out to see her, about ten days after the incident, the baby had already – from what I accrued from news reports – been brought back home to recuperate. Therefore, sometime in the first week of February, I made my way to Netaji Subhash Place Police Station in northwest Delhi, and met with the IO and additional sub-inspector, Parvati. We'd spoken on the phone and I wanted to meet her to find out about the latest developments; I had been given to understand that she was in charge of the investigation on the baby's rape.

Parvati informed me that Suraj, the accused in the case, had been arrested and was currently in police custody. He had confessed to committing the crime under the influence of alcohol. A chargesheet hadn't been filed yet, although she expected to get to it within the next few days – the chargesheet wouldn't be filed for another few weeks after our conversation. The fact that the case had excited public frenzy and caused several talking heads, at once, to bay for the accused's blood, had understandably helped hurry the police proceedings. Parvati, I think, was the first to tell me what the baby's parents did for a living, 'She's a domestic worker and cleans houses in the neighbourhood, and he's a *mazdoor* (daily-wage labourer),' she said and then offered me the father's phone number.

So many months later, as I document this story from its beginning, I marvel at how little we know about the turns things can take and how, at the time I made my delicate phone call to the father of an eight-month-old rape survivor, I had no way of knowing it was merely the precursor to a series of many far less cagey, far friendlier phone calls for years to come.

I made the call, navigated tiny gullies that criss-crossed each other, like the appendages of a many-legged octopus, and found myself getting sucked deeper and deeper into its belly. Finally, I discovered the address that the father had given me over the phone: a two-storeyed house in the middle of a lane of similar-looking houses, each oppressively leaning into the next. There opened a now-familiar green door and I made my way up two flights of stairs to the now-familiar landing inside. While Pia's family lives in a tiny one-room living space, shared among four people, the room does open out onto a generous landing with a decrepit jute charpoy, an old cooler and enough space for Pia and her toddler sister to play in.

At the time, on that February afternoon when I walked in, this tiny one-room house was teeming with people. In fact, before I could even discern who her parents were, a motley group of women from the Delhi Commission for Women's (DCW) local chapter, greeted me, and having heard I was 'press', proceeded to tell me everything that had been accomplished in the case so far. In the midst of the hullabaloo, I noticed the baby's father – quiet but by no means laconic; polite to everybody but keeping his eyes glued and his hands firmly latched on to his little girl.

Once the women had left, I saw the four of them for the first time: a small, thin man, an equally diminutive woman, the baby swathed in bandages in her lap and a vivacious toddler whose laugh sounded almost out of place in the midst of her family's sombreness. I was touched, immediately, by their warmth, for neither mother nor father had any need to do so much as even look my way, that afternoon and yet, they both launched into interrogations about how easy or hard it had been for me to find their house and whether I would like to partake in their tea. I looked at the baby in the young mother's lap and at that first glance, saw only miles and miles of gauze, tape and bandage. Entire walls of the tiny room were lined with bales of cotton and medicinal gauze stuffed into polythene bags, and my heart ached to realize why.

Pia's father, his eye following mine as it mapped the room filled with his baby's supplies, was the first to speak. '*Uss haramzaade ne yeh kiya hai, didi. Main usko kabhi nahi chhodunga* (That bastard did this. I won't spare him).'

There was silence after he had spoken and I sat next to his wife. The attention of the three people in the room was taken up entirely by the tiny bundle nestled in its mother's lap. Had she slept at all? 'Last night, she slept for a total of one hour,' said her mother; her name was Rakhi, she said. Rakhi moved ever so cautiously with her baby in her arms, so as not to wake her or cause her any more harm. 'She's been in excruciating pain for days – the pain keeps her up. Last night, she cried and cried, and wouldn't stop. We didn't know what medicines or what amount of medicine would get her to stop.'

I looked at the eight-month-old, who was, at this point, almost nine months old, but as is often the case with media-driven monikers – like the one that emerged in 2012 – and public imagination, certain names just stick. For the rest of my reporting journey and for ease of reference in future stories, I and the entire media fraternity continued to call her 'the eight-month-old baby', not unwittingly keeping the memory of the brutality against her alive.

I looked at her and felt my stomach turn at the thought of the torment and agony that a puny creature like her had felt, and evidently was continuing to feel. What had happened that Sunday when 'everything went wrong', as Madhav, the father, was now saying, over and over again, as he rocked back and forth in some sort of quiet desperation?

## II

'I LEFT HOME AT ABOUT ELEVEN IN THE MORNING FOR work. I had a couple of homes to clean and returned at approximately at 12:30 p.m. My husband had left home an hour before I did, for his daily gig at a construction site,' narrated twenty-two-year-old Rakhi. 'We had no worries because we'd often left the children in the care of our relatives. My husband's extended family lives in the same house.' Incidentally, Madhav's two older brothers and their families live on the floor below theirs, while his nephew, Suraj, lives in a room directly above. 'And my sisters-in-law have always tended to our kids.' Rakhi and Madhav's engagement of their relatives in childcare, in fact, is representative of most joint family residential setups in India – even those not as indigent as them – where nuclear groups within larger families occupy different floors of the same house and look out for each other's kids, among other things.

That Sunday, when Rakhi returned, however, she knew that something was amiss. 'I'd just entered the gully where our house is, when I saw Suraj, my husband's twenty-eight-year-old nephew, casually ambling in the street. As soon as he saw me, he said, "*Chachi, aap kaha jaati rehti ho? Bachhi ro rahi thi.* (Aunty, where do you keep running off to? Your baby was crying.)"' Surprised at the arbitrariness of his comment, Rakhi said

she retorted by saying, '*Toh, ro rahi thi toh kya hua?*
*Bachhe toh rote hain.* (How does it matter if she was
crying? Babies cry all the time.)' But something didn't
seem right.

Rakhi said she hurried up the stairs to the room, and
claimed that the first thing she saw was her two-year-old
daughter teetering on the doorstep and wailing at the
top of her lungs, as she waddled about in the spacious
landing outside their room. Rakhi could feel her heart
stop and her blood go cold, 'Because at this point, I
could hear far more gut-wrenching cries from within. I
ran inside to see Pia in the middle of the bed, lying in a
large pool of blood and excrement. I started to scream.'

Rakhi remembered gathering her wits and rushing to
the landing to shout for Suraj. 'Suraj, Suraj!' she cried
out, her voice rent with desperation. Rakhi said that
when she saw Suraj walking up the stairs towards her,
she almost charged at him, but Suraj averted his gaze
and mumbled words she couldn't hear. 'I kept asking
him, "*Suraj, tu aaya tha kya? Humare kamre mein aaya
tha?* (Suraj, did you come to our room?)"' But Suraj
muttered something incoherently about calling his wife
on the phone and I began to shout even louder now,
"Why do you need to call your wife? Why don't you
answer my question?"'

Eventually, Suraj managed to slip away in the ensuing
confusion, disappearing up the single flight of steps to
his room upstairs, as Rakhi's sister-in-law clambered up
the steps towards her and looked curiously at the sight
of her bloodied baby. 'She looked intently at the pile of

stool and blood the baby was lying in and said, matter-of-factly, "*Yeh toh latrine kar rakhi hai, aur kuch nahi.* (She's just relieved herself, it's no matter.)" My other sister-in-law went on to tell me later in the day, "*Tujhe kaam karne ki kya zarurat hai? Madhav kamata nahi hai kya?* (Why do you need to go out to work? Does Madhav not make enough money?)"'

These words would continue to rankle me for a long time – for as long, in fact, as I've known Rakhi and plumbed the depths of that morning with her.

I wondered how Rakhi withstood it all – attempting to hold on to the last smithereens of self-control, long enough to get her baby to safety. How it must have felt to realize, inalterably, that her child was not even safe in the one place she'd thought was the safest of all – her own home?'

Eventually, she gathered up her two daughters, called her husband from her cellphone and rushed, at first, to the house of a kindly affluent woman in the neighbourhood where she cooked and cleaned. That woman, Rakhi said, took one look at her baby and pronounced gravely that she should take her to the nearest clinic. It was here that the *mohalla* doctor performed one near-perfunctory examination and, in grave concern, directed Rakhi to the police station without delay.

'The doctor did the dressing for my baby for the time being and I ran to Netaji Subhash Place Police Station, which was closest to me. I feel like everyone knew before

I could even say the words out loud; before I could even think them, that my baby had been raped.'

A First Information Report or FIR was subsequently lodged by ASI Parvati, under the POCSO Act of 2012 and other relevant sections of the Indian Penal Code (IPC), and under her diligent eye and watchful care, Rakhi's baby was admitted to the nearby Kalavati Saran Children's Hospital for treatment. She was sobbing the whole way, but in her own words, was also seething in anger. 'I knew it was Suraj,' she insisted that afternoon. I have asked her many times, since, what made her so sure before his eventual confession and a medical exam proved her worst fears true? 'The way he was ambling in the gully and couldn't look me in the eye. Also, he was drunk.'

At this point, Madhav piped up – a soft-spoken young man who'd slouched in a corner, listening silently all this while, saying nothing – until he mustered up the strength to say valiantly and unexpectedly, 'I don't blame the alcohol, madam. *Peete toh sabhi hai ... maine bhi pee hai.* (Everybody drinks ... I, too, have often drank.) but nobody loses themselves in this manner to do such an abominable thing. When the police later came for him, he kept insisting that he had done it, but only under the influence of liquor. You tell me, madam, can intoxication ever be an excuse?'

To ears and senses accustomed to, and deadened by, the rape apologia issued by cisgender men and ministers for sexual violence (of which 'boys will be boys' is perhaps the choicest staple), Madhav's words struck me dumb. How did a quiet, unassuming thirty-year-old father who kept his shoulders slumped and his opinions to himself, speak with such sterling assurance of the inexcusability of rape – something that even powerful figures and men in academia often fail to understand? He was drunk, he had said. Yet Madhav had torn his story down to nothingness.

The case of the eight-month-old baby had, by this time, escalated to even more frenzied heights. Suraj was arrested in the investigation headed by ASI Parvati, when he confessed and was taken into police custody – all on the same day as the registration of the FIR. The issue was taken up by the Delhi Commission for Women (DCW) chairperson, Swati Maliwal, who tweeted out her anguish, saying, 'The worst has happened ...'[1]

She also arranged for what the family perhaps needed the most at the time – money – and sent Pia's family a cheque for ₹50,000. She wasn't the only one; the Supreme Court directed a further allotment of ₹75,000 to the family and the provision for free medical treatment at the All India Institute of Medical Sciences (AIIMS). The Supreme Court, in fact, acted admirably and swiftly, and just three days after the rape, on 31 January 2018, heard a PIL filed by an advocate, Alakh Alok Srivastava, to state, on record, that it was 'very much concerned' by the rape.[2] The plea asked for an immediate compensation of ₹10 lakh for the family and for the Centre to ensure crimes against minors reached completion of trial within six months of the FIR being filed.

The Supreme Court bench was headed by then Chief Justice of India Dipak Misra. At the Court's directive, Pia – then critical – was visited by doctors from AIIMS-Delhi. Pia underwent a three-hour corrective surgery at the Kalavati Saran Children's Hospital before she was eventually transferred to AIIMS, where she underwent two more surgeries. After spending several days at the hospital, she was released.

All of this, as you may well understand, happened in the whirlwind of the first fortnight, amidst the furore of incensed public opinion, multiple podium speeches and numerous political pleas. For Rakhi, Madhav and the two girls, though, the fortnight moved like a kaleidoscope of blurred images that they could hardly tell apart from one another.

At this time, as I sat opposite them, hearing them recount everything that I had read, Pia had been brought home from hospital and public opinion was still invested in the case – Rakhi and Madhav were hopeful that this meant Suraj would be kept away from their daughters for a long, long time.

He should be hanged, in fact, was what Rakhi said to me then.

### III

I WANT TO MAKE A CLEAN BREAST OF SOMETHING – if there's one thing that truly governs me, post the covering of a rape case, it's guilt. An inordinate amount of soul-crushing, bone-splitting guilt. I wish I could say that the only reason I stay friends with a survivor long after the case is reported and filed away, and much of public/media memory has dissipated, is because of pure, unadulterated friendship. But it is mostly, and largely, always a weighted sense of responsibility, fuelled by guilt which is responsible. Guilt for having asked them questions and for having reported their travails and tribulations, as they navigate their way around the legal process. Once the 'media glare', as one would put it, begins to dim, however, I feel with ever stronger purpose, that I should stay – now more than ever. Surely, after having asked them so many intimate details about their life and following them doggedly to court day in and day out like a spectre, I should stick around for as long as they'll have me?

I should stick around, I think, to ask what their daily life is like now and to examine its vagaries for myself. I should call and text them on most occasions I remember, and return calls and respond to texts at every one of those times. I should do this, I think, to ensure that they don't think of me as someone who ingratiated themselves to them for a while and then slunk into anonymity, leaving them to fend for themselves. These chances are not to be taken for granted, and many times, our correspondence peter down to a trickle and then to nothingness, leaving me to reflect on their quiet and natural death, alone.

On rare occasions, however, they'll go the extra mile. Long, languid and luxuriously buoyant friendships would then be born as a result of the grim, sordid storytelling. This is how it started for Pia, her family and I. It was early in the year of 2018; within the first couple of months after her rape.

It would've been alright to write from home or from the office and make phone calls/reporting trips only every once in a while, when a development emerged. But I found myself making excuses to fill in spaces between those 'essential' trips with non-reporting trips of my own, to visit them. Rakhi and Madhav were predominantly responsible – they were warm to such an inexplicable degree that they invited me over, each time, with a different temptation; a plate of chicken rice on a Sunday, 'the kids miss you', 'we thought of you today', 'those photographs from our India Gate trip are here'.

In the month of February, I shot a documentary on the family, highlighting the immediate perils that the child faced in terms of medical emergencies, and through that documentary (for *The Quint*), exhorted readers/ viewers to donate towards their medical needs and Pia's future education. We'd set up a crowdfunding campaign with the seasoned crowdfunding platform, *BitGiving*, capping our target at ₹5 lakh.

I'll never forget that first weekend. The campaign went live on a Friday. By the time Monday morning rolled around, it had smashed through the cap and was showing no signs of ceasing. That target was raised to ₹10 lakh, which was yet again exceeded within a week. Our final target, born out of sheer perplexity and growing wonder at the perspicacity of our donors, who were spread across the entire length and breadth of India and, by their own admission, from countries far beyond, was ₹15 lakh. The campaign closed at close to ₹12 lakh, raised within a month and built on contributions ranging from a hundred rupees to a lakh, attributable to a string of faceless, nameless donors.

The money was raised and a particular State Bank of India branch near Pia's home became our point of contact; its branch manager, Vandana, our gracious point person. Together, we pored over sheaves of documents that hadn't existed before and that we had coaxed out of reluctant bureaucrats at Aadhar centres across the city, to generate the baby's bank account (marvelling all the while at how adversities forge unlikely fellowships). When Vandana was transferred out of that tiny, near-decrepit branch in the middle of nowhere, a couple of months later, I truly missed her and her no-nonsense barks of '*Kya matlab baby ka account abhi khula nahi?* (What do you mean, the baby's account isn't up and running yet?)' at her lackeys to get things done. In the weeks succeeding the event of the account opening, I would usher in Rakhi and Madhav, too, into that tiny SBI branch, figuring out the technicalities of the fund disbursement, together with Vandana.

Many follow-up stories on the family continued, because I couldn't stop mapping the trajectory of Pia's story after just the one, but none of them truly encompassed the early days of friendship we (her family and I) manufactured during the hospital vigils and long bank queues.

# IV

ONE OF THE PRIMARY WAYS FOR WHICH RAKHI AND I
connected was over language. Sometime, during one
of her early interviews with me, she used 'Sha' far too
often and liberally in lieu of 'Sa' – it was too familiar a
syllabic fallacy for my ears to not perk up immediately. I
asked her if she was Bengali and the diminutive twenty-
two-year-old woman said that she was, indeed, and
that her parents lived in east Kolkata, surprisingly not
too far from where my own lived. Agog, curious and
excited to unravel this new thread, we spoke to each
other, henceforth, largely in Bangla, with a smattering of
Hindi punctuating our sentences, like good non-resident
Bengalis who'd grown used to *Dilli*.

One of the more amusing aspects of this friendship
used to be Madhav's irritation – or at least, the irritation
which was reported to me by a delighted, giggling
Rakhi, 'He always wants to know what we've been
talking about, after I've hung up the phone on you. He
thinks I've been badmouthing him.' Truth is, we spoke
about precious nothing beyond Pia's latest surgery, but
Madhav's newfound insecurity was a source of great
mirth for both of us.

I was more astonished, however, when over the
course of time, the thirty-year-old Madhav became more
of a confidante to me than even my linguistic comrade,
Rakhi. There was something about Madhav's softness
towards his two little children, his refusal to ever use
words like 'shame' and 'family' and 'honour' when he

spoke of his baby – words one heard intoned far too often by fathers and husbands at the site of a rape – and insistence, instead, on education and learning more about fiscal investments to make said education happen, that really impressed me.

Not very many survivor families in my ambit had spoken of the crime as something dissociated from the 'stigma' they'd been conditioned to see in it, but both Madhav and Rakhi, in their unusually quiet ways, performed this dissociation with great finesse. They looked at it for what it was: a cognizable, punishable offence. Nothing more. Nothing less.

The first time we really got along, though – outside of the world inhabited by Rakhi and my easy Bengali platitudes – was the time we said almost nothing to each other for three days in a row.

## V

PIA'S FIRST SURGERY WAS SCHEDULED FOR 17 APRIL 2018. Her mother and father had known about, dreaded and anticipated this date for two and a half months. Within a week of knowing them, I, too, had come to.

This was her first surgery post the flurry of hospital visits and that one long period of internment at AIIMS in early February; the first to determine whether her little body could function on its own in the future and whether the temporary reparations had stood the test of time.

The rape and force on her body had caused a perineal tear – a laceration in her vaginal and rectal wall, causing her to urinate and defecate from the same 'opening' for several days after it happened. Doctors at AIIMS had sealed the laceration, and created an artificial opening in her lower abdomen for stool to pass. For two months, therefore, whenever I visited and sat next to Rakhi as she held a heavily swathed and bandaged Pia in her arms, the latter would be prone to sudden fecal excretions erupting out of her stomach. The eruptions filled me with consternation, anger and wonder – as Rakhi and Madhav rushed about, almost on auto-pilot, shuffling through the latest bale of cotton and gauze, scooping up excreta, applying fresh bandages and lulling the baby to sleep.

They cleaned her twenty to twenty-five times a day, at the time, often in front of me, and I watched the process Rakhi and Madhav had meticulously perfected. Often, there wouldn't be enough room to stack their utensils, since much of the space would be occupied by two segments of cotton – fresh and newly bought and used and ready to be discarded.

'What did he gain?' Madhav muttered, over and over again, as the only acknowledgement of my presence while the baby kicked its legs in my direction.

So here we were, finally, two and a half months later, waiting in the paediatric chambers of the All India Institute of Medical Sciences, for doctors to seal that artificial opening, once they'd determined that her normal functions could be restored. It was no mean feat.

When I look back on the week that I can summarize as the 'Surgeries Week', I marvel at how it had seemed so much longer. Technically, it *had* been longer, since it was after we had been told it would take a day or day and a half at most, that the waiting, watching and ultimate homecoming took us close to a week.

Pia's parents were told, when they appeared with baby and toddler in tow on 17 April, that they would examine her first and then fit her into a slot. Rakhi went in with her, while Madhav, two-year-old Pari and I waited outside. An hour later, Rakhi emerged to say, 'They'll operate on her the day after tomorrow. But she gets admitted to the ward today.'

And so it began. Rakhi stayed back with the baby in the ward for the next couple of days, while the three of us proceeded to say our goodbyes. Madhav wasn't allowed in, so he hugged his child goodbye at the door and then pressed his face to the glass of the ward as he watched his wife and baby settle in. When I left, promising to return the next morning, I looked back and could still see the back of Madhav, lopsided with the weight of his two-year-old on one of his shoulders, staring through the glass.

Madhav, I had begun to understand, was a timid father, often a passive participant in decisions he was too frightened to take – a far cry from the equally diminutive Rakhi, who had begun to embody maternal vengeance and sitting in on every one of Pia's medical examinations, down to this last one.

Somehow, the time spent within the labyrinthine corridors of AIIMS seemed to exist within an alternate time capsule, and every day, for a week, the minute I entered through the doors, pushed in by a throng of impatient people, I forgot that the world outside existed.

For one, the father of the baby who had been raped and I had many meaningful conversations. I remember how we spoke about Kathua and the eight-year-old girl who had been gang-raped only months ago. The incident had sparked a feral rage in young Madhav, who'd keep arguing, 'Why doesn't the government say anything? Why is Modiji so silent? This is no country for girls!'

Over and over, he would say this to himself – sometimes, to me – and then relapse into agonized silence.

Our most unexpected conversation, however, came from an unexpected source. We were watching Pari hop and ferret about in the paediatrics corridor, as we sat on our haunches on the floor. Pari, ever-laughing, ever-mobile, was attempting to vigorously claw off a shiny bead attached to the sandal of a burqa-clad old woman – who had to laughingly fight off her advances and tell her that, sadly, the beads weren't detachable. Laughing all the same, Pari had run up to the front of the corridor and was now looking up the pant leg of someone who looked like a doctor; he bent down indulgently and asked her what her name was. But Pari only smiled. He then handed her a coloured pen and a sheet of paper and she shrieked in delight and ran back to us.

'*Tu bolne kab lagegi, beta?* (When will you start to speak, child?)' Madhav asked her sadly, as he scrunched the curls on her head, interlacing his fingers between them. She looked up at him in intrigue, punched his cheek with a fist and then bobbed her head to continue scribbling the indecipherable squiggles that she was now drawing on the sheet.

I had noticed in the past couple of months, how Pari laughed more than she talked in response to questions directed at her, but hadn't thought much of it. But now, Madhav was telling me about his deepest fear about his elder daughter. 'She's almost two and a half years old, and she does not talk.'

'Are you worried it might be a speech impairment?' I asked him.

'I wasn't before,' Madhav confessed. 'We went to see the doctors, last year – before *this* happened to Pia – and they said some kids just speak late; that she'll probably start talking by age two. But she's almost two and a half, and all she can utter are some incomprehensible sounds. Under any other circumstances, perhaps I would be slightly less worried, but it's the timing, Didi. Look what happened to my little one. *Darr lagta hai ki agar chhoti ke jaise badi wali ke saath bhi aisa kuch ho gaya toh? Woh kaise batayegi mujhe, ki Papa, mere saath kisi ne galat kiya hai? Bolti toh nahi hai*! (I'm afraid – what if someone hurts my elder daughter, too, like they did my younger one? How will she find the words to come and tell me that Dad, someone has hurt me? She doesn't say anything!)'

Pari looked up at the slightly louder inflection of tone that her father had used, and smiled wordlessly.

# VI

MADHAV AND I WERE BACK, THE NEXT MORNING, AND then the morning after the next.

It was purportedly the '*opreshan wala din*', but as it turned out, it still wasn't time.

I was at AIIMS before Madhav got there, and as I waited outside the OPD, Rakhi stepped out suddenly to 'show' Pia to me. 'They put her in these pretty blue hospital robes. Doesn't she look pretty?' She did, like a china doll, I thought, screwing up her nose and scratching her tummy, inside those all-too-large-for-her clothes.

Pia's blood had been drawn, early in the morning, and her haemoglobin was found to be too low to sanction the operation, so it had been moved to 25 April, after a series of precautionary glucose doses. Rakhi and Pia would have to return, a couple of days before the surgery.

It wasn't quite visiting hours yet, but Rakhi snuck me in and I waited by their bedside. Madhav called up, soon, to tell us he was running late because his wife's mother was visiting and he had to go pick her up at the station. Pari was to be left behind with her, to be babysat. I realized that I was missing her tinny squeaks – the only semblance of joviality in this otherwise sepulchral chamber of phenyl and gloom.

Then, Madhav added, '*Main toh nahi aa paya jaldi, par mujhe achha laga ki aap the meri jagah* (I couldn't make it on time, but I'm glad you were there in my place.)'

I felt a strange rush of camaraderie.

Because of all the daily resignation to waiting when the morning of the surgery finally rolled around, Pia's parents were, thankfully, much calmer now. I sneaked in once again, a couple of hours before the surgery, to take a look at her. Pia looked absolutely pristine, holding on to her mother in a vice-like grip, tiny strands of hair slicked back like a little rockstar.

'Very clean and soft,' I tried to explain to Madhav, outside the ward. He smiled, 'She hasn't taken a bath in almost three months now, didi. We only wiped her off with a cloth and changed her bandages.'

He told me how she would howl in pain through the night, those first few weeks. '*Aankhon mein aansun aa jate the, didi. Kaise nahi aate?* (I would burst into tears; how could I not?)'

Madhav had found a place for us to wait, outside the OPD, in a proximal corridor filled with family members and friends of people who were waiting to be operated on. As I took my place among them, I realized I had never waited for anyone for this long in a hospital ward, before. Madhav and I took turns buying water bottles from the AIIMS entrance – a seven-minute walk – while the one who stayed behind, handled the unenviable task of reining in Pari.

For the most part, we sat in companionable silence – a silence punctuated merely by the clinical sounds of the opening and shutting of steel *dabba*s all around us, in the corner, as waiting mothers passed around foil-wrapped, ghee-streaked parathas to waiting, restless children. Apart from that and the sounds of people eating, we had been left to our own devices as we waited for a single word from Rakhi.

It came soon enough. She called to let me know that the surgery was about to begin; it was 3:45 p.m. I communicated the information to Madhav, who attempted to pass it on to Pari, who looked up, once and then vanished into the potpourri of squiggles and scribbles she'd drawn on store-bought sheets of paper. '*Kalaakar hai ekdum* (She's a true artist),' said Madhav fondly, as he placed her on his lap and prepared to wait, like he had been doing for many months now.

'I look around me now, didi, and I see no one. Do you know that three months ago, when all of this happened, there were people galore who promised to stand with us, help us and be there for us, every second of the day? Now that I look around me, I see no one. I guess people forget,' Madhav mused, before relapsing into silence.

I cast an involuntary glance around me. I couldn't see anyone either.

The couple of hours felt like days. Sometimes, we talked, when Madhav wondered aloud what it would be like to return to the construction block, wielding hammer and welding cement, on Monday. Sometimes, we said nothing but I wrote hasty notes in my diary, keeping minutes of the afternoon, and Madhav looked interestedly over my shoulder.

At 5:45 p.m., Rakhi called. It was done.

The moment felt oddly disjointed. The act of anti-climactically relaying the news of surgery when I got off the phone call, as we sat quietly in a waiting corridor, a lonesome twosome – and Pari – felt at odds with the tumult of the journey to get there. I thought it would feel like a raucous, joyful culmination. I'd thought it would feel over.

It didn't.

There was no blessed catharsis waiting to be had, at the end of the tunnel. When I turned to Madhav and asked him, 'It's over, bhaiyya, aren't you glad?' he only said, with his head slightly askew, '*Uski mummy ne bataya bachhi mein teen tube daal di hain ... Ek naak ke andar, shayad saans lene ke liye, aur do dono haathon mein – khoon aur glucose chadhaane ke liye. Itne chhote-chhote haath, didi! Aur naak mein tube! Naak ka nikaal de jaldi ... kitna dard ho raha hoga, na?* (She said there are three tubes sticking out of my baby right now ... One's in her nose, probably to oxygenate, and two others in each of her tiny arms – for blood and glucose. But her hands are so tiny, didi! And a tube in her nose! I hope they take that one out soon, because imagine how much it must be hurting her.)'

It was at that moment that I realized that Madhav had already moved beyond the immediacy of his daughter's surgical success; his mind was probably now lingering on the innumerable future eventualities he and his family would have to consider. The quick battle and the short-lived triumph were not for him; he was already looking into the future.

I think it was also at that moment that I realized my role could now be jettisoned quite reasonably, as Pia's family started to get to their feet to walk to the OPD.

'I'll come back tomorrow to see her,' I promised Madhav, as I stepped out into the New Delhi twilight.

## VII

PIA TURNED ONE ON 6 MAY 2018.

I was invited to her birthday and I turned up with a periwinkle blue dress bought at the baby section of a department store, which turned out to be two sizes too big for her.

Yet, Rakhi was kind enough to quickly put her into it, so I could take a photograph – and for this, the bewildered one-year-old baby was dangled lopsided in her mother's arms, as she drowned under the weight of the dress.

To this day, if I have ever lunched or dined with Rakhi and Madhav at their house, Rakhi has whipped up her favourite concoction of succulent chickpea curry and white rice, which is also my hot favourite. When I put myself on a near-murderous workout regimen, sometime that year, her home was still the only place where I would eat mountains of white rice and sickeningly sweet tea, without complaint. In any case, one's complaints were met with deaf ears and a quickened and more aggravated serving of curry.

There was also the time I took my partner across town to meet them. I'd never been more nervous. He'd said he'd love an introduction, and so I took him, wondering all the way there how 'boyfriend' translated into something benign and non-discomfiting. Ultimately, random words were strung together in lieu of an introduction and their wan smiles told me they got the message.

I had been asked over for Rakshabandhan, a festival that I never celebrate, on account of having no brothers, and having grown up with 'Bhai phota' (its Bengali equivalent, where dots of sandalwood are streaked across foreheads in place of threads around the wrist), instead. But Madhav had said things that were irrefutable, when he'd called, 'My sisters and I haven't been talking for years now. They didn't even visit Pia in the hospital or ask about her after the rape, and now I'd like to believe I have no sisters by blood. If it's alright, I'd like you to be my sister and celebrate Rakshabandhan with us.' Therefore, I had come, bearing a rakhi that I'd bought online and had watched in wonder as Madhav marvelled at the shiny contraption on his wrist like he'd never seen one before, while my friend, Rakhi, insisted on ladling out more *chhole-chawal* than usual, thereby lulling me into an indolent stupor and the conclusion that my life and the friendships it had given me were pretty good.

In all of this, and indeed on many successive visits, the money was never spoken of, unless I brought it up and I would insist on bringing it up. Money had been raised *for* them, through a crowdfunding campaign; why weren't they attempting to use it? But they only said, as they continue to do, '*Abhi zarurat nahi hai, didi* (We don't have any need for it right now).' Madhav would only noncommittally say, 'ATM card *banana chahiye ... hum karlenge, didi* (We should get an ATM card made ... we'll get to it).'

I only remember the chapter of fundraising for Pia, though, through the vagaries of an extremely surreal evening. I'll never forget how I felt – as if some sort of cosmic connection had been unearthed; as though it had always existed and I had only just discovered it.

I had visited Vandana, the SBI branch manager, at the bank nearest to Pia's home, the day before she was transferred out. It was a sombre evening, because she was handing over every document in her possession, which was related to Pia and that she thought someone else must have a copy of, with a flourish of finality. I felt like I was losing a frontline comrade in the battle we were forging with this family. Vandana lived nearby, and after we'd exchanged farewells, she asked if she could drop me to the nearest metro station.

It was late on a weekday evening, so I agreed and we got into an auto. A couple of minutes later, the auto took a circuitous route I had never taken before – usually, I exited Pia's house and the SBI branch, which was right across the road, via the main road. But today, the autorickshaw had found a shortcut through a back alley.

With a jolt, I realized I was facing the road that led down to the railway lines near Nidhi's house; by motorable distance, they were only five minutes apart!

There was something momentous about the geographical manoeuvrings of that evening, which stunned me into silence.

I had believed them to inhabit two entirely distant universes – distanced by the years that separated their rapes. It felt like too much of a coincidence to me that both children, whose stories I had been covering for so very long and whose homes I periodically visited – never once together – lived this close to each other. Would they be friends if they met? I found myself wondering. Would the mothers chat and the fathers sit together in companionable silence? Would their families find kindred spirits in one another?

The discovery felt so portentous that I began to consider doing something I'd never even considered before – speak to one survivor's family about the other. Despite knowing that NGOs, activists, lawyers, policewomen and men did this all the time, I'd shied away from mentioning one's case to another. I'd felt, perhaps, that it would induce unfair comparisons.

Yet suddenly, here I was, telling Madhav and Rakhi what I had discovered – that not so far from them, lived another little girl who had been raped and who was fighting for justice indefatigably. I had made the right decision. Madhav and Rakhi looked at me in wonder and asked a hundred questions, 'How old is she? How old was she when it happened? Is she happy? Who does she live with? Did she know the man who did it? Was he arrested? Is her court case ongoing? When will it end? Will Pia's take as long?'

For the better part of the last two years, that is between 2018 and 2020, Pia's parents have quizzed me about what I think is an approximate timeline in the POCSO courtroom, which is hearing their baby's rape case. They ask me how long they think it will be till Suraj is jailed for life. Then they tell me, in the form of platitudes that seem directed at themselves more than at me, 'After all, it won't be too long. It can't be. Everyone knows he did it. It's open and shut.'

I've often tried to tell them about the vagaries of law, about the inordinate delays of our police and justice systems, while also reminding them of their being on the right side of that law and of being assured justice. Except that that justice, I coax them into understanding, probably won't be at the *agli tareekh* that they vouch for, to each other, and to me.

But perhaps, nothing I'd ever said had quite the same impact as the story of Nidhi – a story they could relate to and understand. They heard it like one whose crests and troughs resembled those of their own, and in the end, when I tentatively suggested, '*Kabhi baat karna chahoge unki mummy se?* (Would you ever wish to speak to the child's mother?)' I'll ask if she can explain it all to you', both Rakhi and Madhav looked like they were seriously deliberating over the prospect.

Maybe, one day, they'll make that phone call.

# VIII

THE FIRST COURT HEARING FOR PIA'S CASE THAT I attended was actually her second, and it took place in early October 2019.

Her parents were nervous.

They had called me, the night before, to ask if I would accompany them. '*Ho sakta hai kal hi saza mil jaye* (It's possible that the culprit will be sentenced tomorrow),' Madhav said confidently, and I hesitated to communicate the unlikelihood of that possibility to him.

I reminded them, though, of Nidhi's case – a sad reminder of the sluggard Indian justice system – pointing at the two and a half year long trajectory thereafter, and Madhav thought for a moment and then said, '*Humare case mein nahi lagega, didi. Jald hi suna denge.* (That won't happen in our case. They'll sentence the man sooner.)' I wasn't sure what to say to that, so I said nothing.

A day in the courtroom for Madhav, Rakhi, Pari and Pia is an entire event. The kids are shaken out of their beds earlier than usual, bathed under a tiny tap in a corner of their landing, and squeezed into frocks bought especially for 'outings', as Madhav calls them. They, then, fasten more locks than the average goldsmith to their door – the parents no longer trust the families enough to leave their home unguarded – and hail an auto or clamber on to a Tis Hazari-bound bus, whichever comes first. Then, they navigate their way through cold, bustling, unfeeling labyrinths of corridors, until they find the right door, marked with the number they have been given over the phone. Finally, they sit – for hours – on a bench just outside the door, waiting for their turn. Their lawyers have told them it could be any minute after the stipulated hour, and Rakhi and Madhav don't want to lose a minute.

It was here, on the date of their second court hearing, that I met them – a quiet foursome, dressed in new sets of clothes and perched patiently on one long wooden bench, sanguine in their collective hope for justice. It was 11 a.m.; the public prosecutors presenting their case had said they'd call for them at noon.

'*Aaj hi ho jayega, didi*, (It will all be done today)' Rakhi and Madhav chirruped. But did they know what their hearing was going to entail? They did not. I waited for one of the prosecutors to bob her head out of the door to tell them they'd be wanted in twenty minutes and asked her, 'Is the judge hearing testimonies?' 'Only Suraj's family's. The accused's wife wants to ask for bail.' She vanished. I stopped short of relaying the news to the parents who would undoubtedly throw a fit.

For the rest of the time that we sat on that bench, I remained enthralled by the two children – particularly the one we'd come here for. Pia had slid off her mother's lap and landed on the floor with a thump; the folds of her frock now danced up behind her as she set about perambulating the circumference of the waiting hall, balancing on the heels of her feet. She'd appear in front of us for a minute, giggling and pleading our attention, but the moment one of us lunged to scoop her up, she'd run away in the opposite direction, laughing harder each time and hopping on the balls of her feet. Soon, every waiting family with a child in tow – as this was the waiting area 'designated' for the POCSO courtroom-bound – had their eyes fondly trained on this tiny object of attention, who couldn't possibly know that a trial for her rape was underway, mere metres away.

I watched Madhav as he watched her – over the many months that I've known him, this has become one of my favourite things to do. Madhav's young eyes light up with an inexplicable fervour, when he hears his baby's laughter; a fervour quickly tinged with sorrow and rage as he expostulates, '*Uss haraamzade ko toh*!' Rakhi usually remonstrates him with a look at this point and he is silenced.

That morning, however, Madhav's usual verbal imprecations and glibness of tongue were brought up unexpectedly and unfavourably in court. Suraj's defence attorney stood facing the magistrate, with Suraj's defiant young wife and middle-aged mother standing to attention – both biting down on the *pallu* of their sarees between their teeth and refusing to look to their left, where Rakhi and Madhav were casting practised glares at them.

Suraj's attorney staked a claim for bail for his client – his son was sick, he argued, and coughing up sputum. The request was summarily dismissed by the magistrate who wouldn't allow bail on the grounds of a cold.

I listened as public prosecutors refused to be quelled and began to list the crimes Suraj was accused of committing.

I wish Rakhi and Madhav weren't listening to the recounting of the rest – the enumeration of all the various injuries that had been inflicted on their baby; the many ways in which she had been attacked being listed now, with dispassionate precision. But the duo, who stood an inch ahead of me, barely flinched.

'They want him freed, didi,' muttered Madhav under his breath, 'Can you believe it? After what he did to my girl.'

If I thought Madhav was veering dangerously close to losing his temper, I wasn't alone. The defence counsel now continued – clearly, a train of argument that had begun at the previous hearing – that he believed Madhav and Rakhi's request for police protection for themselves and their children was an invalid one. He argued that they constantly butted heads with his client's wife and mother, demanding that they be handed over the property (the house) immediately. The property was the reason they'd accused Suraj of the crime, said his attorney; Suraj, in fact, had committed no crime at all, and had merely frolicked with his niece, ending up hurting her with his fingernails.

The tiny courtroom exploded with cries – largely from Rakhi, but superseded almost immediately by a round of solid table-thumping by her baby's lawyers. They demanded to know how such a contestation could be made at this point, when the man in judicial custody had confessed to the crime, and when multiple medical examinations had already corroborated what Rakhi had said. 'She was raped,' the woman at the forefront of the huddle declared angrily.

She needn't have bothered. The judge that faced both huddles looked in no mood to entertain this latest exposition. There would be no further argument on the state of the child, he told the defence counsel, and stated that he'd understood the contention over police protection.

The public prosecutors spent the rest of the hearing convincing the judge why protection should be provided to the family at all costs, reiterating that the parents were desperate to prevent another crime against their daughter(s). But the judge passed a conciliatory order that both teams of lawyers acquiesced to – a single policeman would be assigned the duty of patrolling Rakhi and Madhav's house twice a week, to make sure everything was alright.

'They were lying, didi,' both mother and father turned to me, when proceedings were adjourned, bringing to an end the now-endless haranguing between the public prosecutor's team and her counterpart's. 'We don't unnecessarily tell them off. They needle us whenever we cross paths on the common staircase, about how we're bringing shame to the family and how we should've withdrawn this case a long time ago. Not one of them was concerned enough to come see Pia at the hospital. And what do I need to demand property for? My father already equitably distributed the whole house among the three of us brothers. I live in a room that's rightfully my own – just like they have theirs. In fact, *they've* been refusing to share a copy of the deed with me.'

I understood, I told him, but insisted he keep his calm. 'You don't want to give them any excuse to launch counter-offensives.'

I wasn't sure if Madhav had heard. Or if he did, the words paled in front of the face of the one-year-old that he now stared at, in palpable agony. I didn't need to ask any questions.

I only told him that I was going to ask the prosecution some questions and raced inside, as the motley crew within the courtroom began to disperse into tinier clusters of ones and twos. I was looking for the woman I had heard earlier, declaring Pia's rape irrefutably and indubitably to the entire courtroom; I found her, still sitting at the bench in front of the magistrate's.

I called out to get her attention, and then stopped short in my tracks.

I was looking at Raj Kataria, the same woman who was fighting Nidhi's case! 'Are you a part of the prosecution?' I asked in amazement, as the middle-aged woman I had met only a few months ago, stared back in pleasant surprise. She stood up to greet me and nodded, 'Yes, are you covering her case?'

I told her I was. What I didn't tell her was how stupefied I was, to find yet another similarity between Nidhi's and Pia's lives. Similarities that seemed to be drawing them closer and closer to each other, even as they remained unaware and oblivious of each other in this chain of otherwise unremarkable events.

Totally oblivious of my stupefaction, she began to explain the nuances of the police protection she had successfully garnered for Rakhi and Madhav, and how the facts of the case remained solid. 'Rock-solid,' she said.

She mouthed a few hopeful pleasantries, I responded with hopeful platitudes, and we parted ways. Possibly until Pia's next hearing. Or perhaps, Nidhi's.

I caught up with Madhav and Rakhi, who were the last stragglers in the now-empty corridor; the girls had gambolled far ahead, making the most of the desolate space and swooping down upon each other in delight. Madhav and Rakhi, for once, didn't seem too concerned about calling them back within bounds; they'd rather hear about whether Ms Kataria and her team had proffered a lead, a date or some proof of expediency in the case; anything they could take back home for keeping up hope. I could offer nothing, but I offered them a ride back home.

'We'll be back soon,' Madhav picked up the thread confidently. 'They were saying next month.'

'So, November?' I asked.

'Yes, this thing is almost at an end anyway,' he chatted, and began to enumerate the lot of totally trustworthy people that were going to provide witness on behalf of Pia, how the judge had looked during each one of the prosecution's arguments and how the medical reports he hadn't quite been able to decipher were surely entirely in Pia's favour.

It didn't quite pan out the way Madhav and Rakhi had convinced themselves it would, though. One cold Saturday in mid-November 2018, I got a call from Madhav, who told me that the 22 November hearing

had been postponed to 30 January 2019. For the first
time, I heard his voice falter. No one would hear from
Pia for two more months. No one would remember her
until she took centre-stage again.

'But I think that'll be it, didi. January 30 to finish
it all.'

## IX

ON AN UNSEASONABLY WARM MARCH AFTERNOON IN
2019, I tiptoed into Madhav and Rakhi's house, unsure
if anyone was at home – no one had made a noise as
I had traipsed up the stairs to their landing. I soon
knew why. The couple sat, gaping open-mouthed at a
cumbrously large LCD in front of them, that covered
most of the dimensions of one wall. Rakhi barely looked
down at the mound of pulao she had gathered in a fist
and dipped into *kaali dal*, and Madhav's fingers were
caked in dried scraps of sabzi, as he let his plate rest on
his knee.

Both were busy looking at the screen, which was
currently showing visuals of a street, distorted by static.
At first glance, I assumed I'd walked in on an intense
television soap opera, when I found them this way. A
closer viewing confirmed my latent suspicions; that they
were glued to the footage their CCTV cameras had
picked up, of the streets.

Madhav and Rakhi are now the unenviable owners of
four closed-circuit television sets: two sit at the top and
bottom of their narrow staircase, and the other two peer

out into the street, transmitting visuals of bystanders occasionally glancing at the camera in puzzlement.

Most days, these past few months, they've whiled away many a morning, adjusting and re-adjusting the faces of the cameras to their satisfaction, then peering into the all-knowing, four-partitioned LCD to nab a who-knows-what. I've asked them several times who they're really hoping to find with their cameras. Madhav and Rakhi haven't felt sure. Sometimes, it's suspicious-looking passers-by who seem to be lurking a little too close to the door. Sometimes, it's the extended family that they don't even trust as far as they could throw a shoe ('They would be up to anything if we didn't keep an eye on them, didi,' they've said darkly). Most times, though, they're just staring at reflections of themselves in the translucent black screen – trepidatious, lonely and wrapped up in blankets and hopes, holding their babies close.

How did they come about getting the screen? Madhav and Rakhi were granted the right to instal these – a policeman who was deputed the task, came by one morning, and fitted them up – post a court hearing I didn't attend, when, once again, a dispute broke out in front of the judge between Pia's parents and the accused's family. The latter declared that the former were instigating squabbles with them; Pia's parents asserted that the people who couldn't protect their daughter – one of whom, in fact, had raped her – could not be trusted and they demanded authoritatively sanctioned state protection. A property dispute was also thrown into the mix, for the judge's auditory pleasure – Madhav and his two brothers had been haggling over quartering their house into equitable parts for years – and now, conspicuously large CCTV cameras had been introduced into the inconspicuous home with the green door, that had caught everyone's fancy.

In the mere space of a year, therefore, the phone calls have sped up rapidly. They come like clockwork, offering little by way of diversity. The calls, often panicked, are made by Madhav who insists that his brother is coming up the stairs to hurt them. Madhav claims he'd like to sell his floor of the house to amass enough money to move out and live away from the microcosm in which his daughter had been violated – but that, apparently, his brothers will have none of it. 'You've already sullied our name, now you want to sever the house, too?' he quotes them as saying.

So they refuse to hand over the papers they claim to have lost, Madhav says, and so, Rakhi and Madhav look unblinkingly at their screen, in a strange sort of delirium, apprehending the next abominable move against them.

One came, a few weeks ago. A number of WhatsApp messages blew up my phone – all of them blurry videos of a man and a woman racing up the stairs as if to break down Madhav and Rakhi's door, both silhouettes cocking their fists at them. The man and the woman look angry – and they look rather like Madhav's older brother and his wife, from the floor beneath theirs. Suddenly, a burlier man appears on the screen and seems to haul the 'offending' man away by the collar with some semblance of authority. Madhav later tells me it is a plainclothes policeman, whom he has called to keep his brother away. It certainly looked scary. What looked scariest, though, on that screen, is the flickering image in its tiniest right-hand bottom corner – the image of a pigtailed four-year-old and her now almost three-year-old baby sister, cowering fearfully from the loud voices and the violence in the adults' gesticulations, trying to make one with the shadows. Pia and her older sister look befuddled.

I looked at Madhav and Rakhi staring at their screen, still, and I understood. This screen is a means to drive a wedge between them and the sordid reality they must inhabit – a safety chasm of their own engineering – to shield them and their daughters from the estranged family they both fear and loathe.

In the midst of all of Madhav's angry soliloquys, the most prominent emotion that comes through is his sadness. They never visited, he reminisces, over and over again, as he talks about the time Pia was in hospital, undergoing surgery, senseless with tubes sticking out of her.

'She was in there for longer than a week and they never came to see her. They didn't even ask. Even my two sisters back home in our *gaon*, kept their distance; my brothers must have told them about Suraj. Every one of them made us feel isolated. How can we not think, then, that they are siding with Suraj?'

Rakhi, in turn, cannot forget the slew of taunts hurled her way – each member of the family blaming her for leaving her daughters alone, daring to venture out to work, conveniently absolving Madhav of having shown any such 'negligence'. The taunts hit their mark. Their patriarchal machinations are writ large on her face as she feverishly sticks by her girls, every waking minute of her life – the last day she went out to work had been on 28 January 2018, the day Pia was raped. Wouldn't she like to return to her job? I press her and her responses range from 'when this is all over' to more considered and far more convincing, soft-spoken admissions of 'yes, but then, what of the children?' Madhav's role seems to have been relegated to a recess in her brain.

~

Rakhi and Madhav, today, continue to live from one court date to another. 'Wouldn't you rather stay somewhere else, even while the trial is going on?' I asked in the initial months in 2018, thinking about how hard it must be, sitting here, listening to the sound of Suraj's wife's footsteps above their heads, as she paces in measured circles around her room, attempting to lull her and Suraj's infant son to sleep.

'One day, we want to move to Kolkata,' Madhav would say, his eyes shining. He had been to his wife's place several times since the rape, viewing the getaway like an escapist's vacation; he'd then bring his wife's sexagenarian mother to live with them in Delhi, so he knew the eastern Indian metropolis well, he said. 'That is a lovely place. There, we will not be living with these relatives. And Pia and Pari will be safe,' he'd declare.

Late in 2019, things seemed to change when Rakhi and Madhav began to talk about moving out; about finding a new home in the northwestern Delhi neighbourhood to rent and live in. Rakhi came close, I thought, when one Sunday, I accompanied her and her two girls (one encased in the nook of her arm, the other clasping her palm) to a building that looked uncannily like their present house. 'What do you think?' she asked in excitement. 'I'm still trying to negotiate prices and see what a good time is, for us to make the move.' She never zeroed in on a house, even as she talked up the safety of the neighbourhoods she'd seen, assured in her decision.

But months of accompanying them on what seem to be wild goose chases has convinced me that, for now, at least, the real estate hunt is a mirage. The very motivations that make them want to move, pull them back. Neither of them wants to bring up their daughters in the home of their girl's alleged rapist and a family who've turned their backs on them. 'I feel stifled here,' Rakhi says in exhaustion. Yet, that same Rakhi is determined to stay put until the trial is well and truly over. 'I don't want to leave until he's been put away,' she expostulates, offering no reason for her ambivalence.

## X

20 MARCH 2020. FRIDAY.

Rakhi calls early. She sounds excited, almost frenetic. 'Did you watch the news?' It is 10 a.m. 'I haven't,' I confess. They've hanged Nirbhaya's rapists, she tells me in a rush. Surely this can mean positive things for her child? That they'll accelerate all rape cases across the board? Expedite judgments fuelled by renewed public interest? The phone moves quickly to Madhav who asks me the same questions, also following up with details of the television coverage he has seen: footage broadcast by reporters stationed right outside the prison where four men were hanged. He'd watched, he said, as TV channels had shown vehicles making way to the crematorium, followed by speeches from activists and lawyers.

I wonder which of the admonitions would seem more timely: a reminder to stay away from loud, rabble-rousing television news, or a sermon on the intricacies of capital punishment in our society, and decided on doing neither. This isn't about either of those things for the duo; it's about the one question they both ask over and over again: 'Nirbhaya's case had reached a verdict – Pia's will, too, won't it?'

Rakhi's pressing insistence that day – as on every other day – is that the trial be over before Pia grows up enough to be able to discern things, to understand what happened to her and how legal machinery has been set in motion to right that wrong. While the insistence and the want to draw hope from Nirbhaya are understandable, they also lay bare the ugly truth of India's leaden justice system. The twenty-three-year-old female physiotherapy student's case had reached a relatively speedy verdict, by Indian legal standards, with four adult defendants handed out convictions only a year later, in September 2013. The fifth adult had died in jail, while in police custody, and the sixth defendant, a juvenile, was sentenced to a reform facility. Yet, appeals rolled on for years, with the executions happening only in 2020. Does Rakhi/Madhav want that long-drawn, gut-wrenching process in Pia's case?

While Pia's case also – like Nirbhaya's – invited public censure, international attention and governmental intervention, it throws up an awful reality – in the story of the Nirbhaya gang rape and murder, there was a 'body'. A body flung from a bus and ignored by passers-by, on a cold December night. A body that eventually succumbed to the heinous assault. A body that embodied both the collective guilt and the collective grief of a country that had slept on rape for decades, until that point. Therefore, things had inspired quicker action than usually seen, in governments and courts. That kind of action in sexual assault cases, sadly, depends on the 'degree' of brutality: how many men were there? What objects did they use? Did she live through the night?

Rape in India impacts Indians differently. It impacts them hardest when it answers to every one of those voyeuristic degrees.

I say none of this, however. I only listen as Rakhi continues chatting on the phone about how she's desperate for the next hearing. They haven't been too frequent in the past two years – despite the 'fast-track' nature of POCSO courts – and Rakhi and Madhav go to court, only every three months or so. 'Do you think the judges will ask us what punishment should be given to

Suraj?' she wants to know. It is unlikely, I tell her, and she sounds disappointed.

Rakhi's insistence on giving even her child's magistrate notes, is characteristic of both her and her husband – from what I've come to know of them, over the years. They will call pretty much anyone who is kind to them and is directly or indirectly involved in Pia's case, as often as they can, eager to hear good news. Often, it is ASI Parvati who is next to testify in court, along with some other members of her investigation team, according to Rakhi and Madhav. Often, it is the lawyers and activists deputed by HAQ Centre for Child Rights to assist the legal process. Under India's federal structure of government and the Juvenile Justice (Care and Protection of Children) Act of 2000, it is the responsibility of the state's Child Welfare Committee (CWC) to appoint an NGO or social worker or any suitable advocate to protect the child's interests in court, during the entire legal proceedings. The advocate, in turn, appoints a lawyer from among their own team, to advise the child during trial. Accordingly, Pia was represented not only by the state through public prosecutors, but also by a team from an NGO, HAQ. The organization had summoned the couple several times, therefore, for psycho-social counselling sessions, and Rakhi and Madhav claim proudly that they have been to every single one of them.

Mention this level of proactiveness to public prosecutor Raj Kataria, and she laughs in agreement.

Pia's parents do not have her number, but she has viewed their enterprising spirits up close in court. 'Pia's mother is the one I interacted with, the most. I can tell you this, *agar unki mother aisi nahi hoti, toh shayad main yeh case aage nahi kar paati* (if her mother wasn't the way she is, then perhaps I wouldn't have been able to take the case to where it is today). Every mother should be like that woman, agitating for *real* justice for her daughter. This, despite the fact that she faced incredible pressure from the family; *sab upar neeche hi rehte hai.* (Everyone in the family lives above or below them.)'

Kataria is no longer on Pia's case – just as she is no longer on Nidhi's – both having been transferred out from under her to a new POCSO courtroom, last year, in October 2019. She'd told me this when we'd spoken of Nidhi's trial developments, but she still remembers much of the early hearings, 'When Rakhi took the witness stand, I believe it took her two entire hearings to finish her statement; that's how much she wanted to say. That statement was punctuated by intermittent tears, but she made it through bravely, and she spoke *so* well. Now, Pia's father, in comparison, was far shier. He got through his statement quite meekly. But the mother ... she's a brave one.'

Kataria remembers also a climacteric moment during the early days of the trial, 'when the *jethani* (the elder sister-in-law) turned hostile'. She was such a crucial witness for the prosecution – she had stood at Rakhi's door and watched Suraj come upstairs, and then flee to his room. That sudden about-face could have caused our case to crumble, but Pia's mother held her own. So did the IO, actually, Parvati. She gathered all the connecting evidence very well.'

I neglect mentioning Raj Kataria's indictment of her sister-in-law to Rakhi, as I know it will only serve to rile up an already incensed mind. But when Rakhi calls again, a week after Nirbhaya's rapists' execution, we speak of the next steps in the trial; according to my conversations with the prosecutor, another few hearings should wrap it up.

'The next hearing is supposed to be on 16 April, but that seems unlikely,' she muses, thinking of the pandemic that has pushed back all court dates. She turns out to be right. India – like several other countries worldwide – announced a nationwide lockdown to counter the coronavirus; this lockdown, in fact, was to be extended a number of times thereafter. Her major concerns with the postponement of the date are that Suraj will find a way to 'make bail'. I try to tell her it isn't easy; that we had, together, witnessed the POCSO magistrate turn down such a request, earlier. While bail is permissible under almost every law of the Indian Penal Code, even section 302 (applicable to murder), it is a lot harder under the POCSO Act, I tell her.

Kataria, when I direct the same question at her, however, does not conciliate. 'I've been practising in POCSO court for seven years, and *jo degree* of sensitivity *pehle dino mein thi, woh ab nahi rahi* (the degree of sensitivity we saw in the early days of POCSO has since disappeared). *Ab toh aisa hai ki* bail *toh ho*

*jayegi bhaiyya, ladki ko chhed diya toh kya ho gaya?*
(now it's like, accused parties believe they'll get bail
really easily, so what if they've harassed women?) Judges
have inculcated too much leniency. I know the papers
report on how difficult it is to be granted bail under the
Act, but generally, courts *mein* judges *ki* thinking *doosri
hai* (judges think otherwise in the courtrooms).'

Kataria, in fact, goes on to list the many recorded
instances when a man, out on bail, has gone on
to commit worse crimes. 'I remember a case I was
prosecuting, where a boy who'd grabbed a girl's hand
was given bail. The judge, when I had opposed the
defence's petition, had told me, "Madam, *haath hi to
pakda hai, ab kya uski jaan loge?* (He only grabbed her
hand, do you want to take his life?)" I said nothing. In
yet another case, a few days later, a teenage girl on her
way to school, was accosted by a boy in the gully and
kissed. When I opposed the bail petition for the boy,
the judge said, "Madam, it's been 15–20 days since he's
been in custody. Think of his age." I told him then, "Sir,
*aisa hai, abhi 3-4 din pehle ek ne haath pakda tha toh
sirf haath hi pakda tha. Aaj is ladke ne kiss kar diya toh
chalo kiss hi toh kar diya* (Sir, here's how I see it: 3–4
days ago, a boy grabbed a girl's hand and we said that
he had only grabbed her hand. Today, this boy has kissed
a girl and we say that he's only kissed her.)" If we're
not careful, we're going to see way worse soon. And the
judge dismissed the application.'

She wishes more judges understood this. 'At the
district court level, their thinking is, "We've got to

dispose of all these bail applications quickly." And the high court says, "don't overpopulate jails". But they need to consider what happens to the families of the survivor, when they release an accused on bail. So many change houses, move localities ... perhaps, judges should hike the bail bond amount or apply conditions, but something does need to be done.'

I tell Rakhi or Madhav none of this in our most recent phone calls during the lockdown. Occasionally, they send videos over WhatsApp of Pia and Pari waddling about happily in the landing, their kiddie shoes making squelching noises. On one occasion, Madhav tells me he is learning to cook *palak ki sabzi* (spinach curry). 'I didn't want to sit idle at home!' he grins. Mostly, both Madhav and Rakhi will hold the cellphone to their girls' ears and exhort them to say 'Hello'. Pia, once 'the eight-month-old baby', now lisps full sentences in a mix of Bengali and Hindi; she asks me to come visit her soon. That, perhaps, is the most momentous indicator of time in the trial of Pia's rape.

# 6

# Smita

## I

IT'S HARD TO MAKE PLANS WITH SMITA AND ENSURE she sticks to them. You could tell her, 'Majnu ka Tilla, 4 p.m.,' and still expect to be called sometime before schedule and hear whingeing to the tune of: 'Actually, mother will be deeply worried if I get too late coming home, didi. Can we do X or Y or Z place, and maybe 3 o'clock instead?'

You grumble and you gripe and, most often, exchange a flurry of petulant words (that you tell yourself you're permitted after a nearly four-year-long friendship), but you agree. And you meet at a point where she feels, well, safe(r).

Plans with Smita hinge on a fulcrum of variables – how 'safe' or 'dangerous' a certain cafe, metro terminal or local watering hole feels to her; whether a certain item of food served by an unsuspecting bearer will potentially trigger a memory or elicit a sob; and whether she can return home by sundown or before her parents chastise her for being 'out' – whichever comes first.

I've asked her a number of times, to let me talk to her parents; to urge them to understand if she needs to go out; or to loosen the safety net they've ensconced her with, but Smita always refuses. 'I've just got them to trust me,' she says emphatically, over and over again. 'They're letting me go, little by little. I don't want to jeopardize this.'

I suspect that Smita doesn't really want to let go of the safety net just yet, either. I suspect she enjoys having it engulf her in a bottomless cocoon, not having to deal with the world until she's ready. I suspect that she continues to believe she caused her own rape – four years and no resolution later.

## II

THERE ARE FAR TOO MANY THINGS – TOO MANY objects and artefacts around the large and labyrinthine city of Delhi that feel too familiar – and therefore, claustrophobic to her. 'We can't meet at Kashmere Gate station!' she vetoes a perfectly run-of-the-mill 'cold coffee and selfies' plan, one Saturday afternoon, in panic. 'We used to meet here. He lives nearby. He could be on the train at this very moment. He could be changing trains. He could be going home. Do you know his home is by the station; down that little gully where the vendors set up shop? Do you see that gully, and the *Ram laddoo* bhaiyya? I wonder if that bhaiyya remembers me from all those times we stopped to buy a plate ...'

There is no end to the vicious loop; to the kaleidoscope of blurred images of a relationship past, that are prompted by the smallest details – inconspicuous to the naked eye, but full of meaning and misery for Smita. Once, after I had known her long enough, I mustered the courage to ask her, 'Do you still love him?' She must have guessed at the mingled sense of surprise and wonder in my voice. Either way, her response seemed rehearsed, like something you say because it's what people would like to hear, 'I remember the good times ... but how can I still love him? How can I think of him fondly, after what he did to me? He discarded me like a used scrap of paper. Like I was nothing.' The reverie is quickly retracted and corrected by a vehement, 'He *should* be punished. Why does he get to walk the streets scot-free while I suffer in silence?'

The ambiguity is marked, but with her, it has always been. If I've known Smita for four whole years now – four years punctuated by perfectly regular, monthly visits to nondescript Cafe Coffee Days – each one of those visits has her teetering on the edge of a precipice. One side beckons her to immerse herself in fractured memories of a relationship that ended in rape. Another, towards willing the man she once loved, to be put behind bars. I can only make conjectures about which side of the precipice she'll let me into, on a given day.

I was sure I knew her mind, when I met her the first time. It was during an interview that had ended with both of us in tears. The cameraperson who'd accompanied me had hastily capped the lens to what had been a rather disastrous shoot which Smita had sputtered and stammered all the way through, periodically and savagely poking at the corners of her eyes to wipe a stray tear. The shoot had then come to a crashing halt, with her collapsing into a heap of tears at the climax of her story and with me rushing to her side, muttering hapless nothings and hissing 'cut it! cut it!' over her head, to my horrified colleague.

Only minutes before, she had been up on a stage, relating some of the rawest and most guttural things I'd ever heard, finishing bashfully only to bask in a sea of resounding applause. Acting on an invitation to listen to her – among other survivors – speak at New Delhi's Constitution Club, I had listened to her in awe. Smita's presence had struck me the minute she'd walked up to the waiting microphone. Even from a few yards away, I could tell she was nervous.

Cowering noticeably under the glare of a couple hundred eyeballs and flashbulbs, which made her appear a little hunchbacked, the petite young woman – who, I later found out, was only a year younger than I was – started to speak. Quelling every other voice, every whisper, every breath in the room, Smita spoke – haltingly at first, then tremulously – of the man who raped her. Twice.

When she finished, I couldn't stop clapping.

I would often ask her, later, where she had found the nerve to do something like that; she, who shrank from the spotlight like a woman possessed.

She hesitated. 'Maybe it was the fact that it was my first time.'

'Your first time talking about what happened?'

'*Haan, ek bar bolna tha. Par maine galat socha tha.* (Yes, I needed to talk about it at least once. But I miscalculated.) That first time hit me like a ton of bricks.'

The first time. I clearly remembered the first time I went up to Smita and asked if she would tell me her story in greater detail, in front of a video camera. I would frame her in a silhouette to mask her identity and distort her voice, if she'd like, I told her. She agreed – which, it would later occur to me, she did to avoid disappointing the woman who'd asked her nicely.

The thought echoed in my head several times, during the rest of her narration.

It was going to be my most defining memory of her.

## III

SMITA ALWAYS TAKES A LONG TIME GETTING TO THE point. So was it then, so is it now.

She began addressing the camera, that afternoon, for instance, with anecdotes of her MCA degree – a saga of unpleasant desk days at her first job and constant exclamations of, 'But I knew I could do more things. Better things! I was going to make something of myself.'

Smita's small chin looked up defiantly as she said, 'I mean, it's not like we had money problems – not like my father ever ... but I knew ... So I joined a call centre.'

This was to be the first of many instances where I realized Smita had trouble finishing a sentence and tended to hurriedly latch on to her next flight of fancy, even before she'd finished articulating the first.

'I'd earned something of a permanent contract at a media conglomerate, but they were going to make me work nights, and my dad was staunchly against night shifts. I had to quit that one.' So, Smita joined a call centre in Sector 62, Noida. And here, she had attempted to make herself at home.

Her first sense of foreboding had sprung from a mysterious source. 'The receptionist I had made friends with, when I had first joined – and who'd been at my interview – suddenly quit, and a new woman called Rachna took her place. I asked her why the former receptionist had quit and a friendly female colleague, called Suman, offered that she'd had personal grievances.'

I couldn't tell if the receptionist's sudden departure had later seemed ominous to her – such a little detail as that – but it has certainly resurfaced in a brain addled with confusing strands of information from those days. What had been real? What was not?

'I eventually became friends with Suman. Do you know, didi, that I've always had more male friends than female? I thought I should give Suman a shot. I also met Karan, not long after. He was one of the team leads in the office, although I wasn't in the team he headed.'

Gradually, her 'friend circle' had begun to widen.

'I didn't know much about ringing people up to ask if they needed insurance, but I was figuring it out. I literally just had to make phone calls, going, "*Kya aapne insurance le rakha hai*? (Do you have insurance?)" And if they said yes, I would transfer the call. *Bas itna sa kaam tha.* (That was the sum total of my duties.) What? Yes, I was making friends, but I should not have been. I should have left after that first week.'

But Smita had been there for a couple of weeks and had even facilitated what she described as an 'office romance'. 'Suman and I would travel together on the metro for some distance and Karan knew we were friends. He asked to be set up with her and they eventually got together. Perhaps, he wanted to return the favour. I wish he hadn't. He introduced me to a colleague I hadn't yet met, Deepak.' Smita faltered.

I looked up uneasily.

'He's the one that assaulted me,' she said steadily, with only a hint of fervour in her voice. There was a second's pause. Then, 'Deepak joined the motley crew of call centre employees who were Delhi-bound from the Noida terminal. Because he lived near Kashmere Gate and I lived further up north, we'd lose most of the office crowd, halfway, at Rajiv Chowk station, where they'd disperse. It'd be just the two of us until it was time for him to deboard.'

Smita spoke of an unexpected happenstance that brought them closer together. 'At the time, a boy from work, called Ajay, had started following me around, occasionally lurking around my cubicle at lunch hours and insisting on dropping me home after work. I sought Karan's help and he casually suggested, "*Tu Deepak ke saath kyun nahi jaati?* (Why don't you go home with Deepak?) He'll ward off the nuisance."'

So a work superior (Karan) had repudiated a subordinate's (Smita's) sexual harassment complaint, while goading her to romance another fellow superior? I wanted to ask her why, but gratitude was slathered large on her face.

Gratitude that someone had offered her the short end of the stick.

As Smita earnestly elaborated on how her Deepak began escorting her out of the metro station, daily, and put her in an autorickshaw home, I asked if he – or anyone in the vicinity, or indeed at her workplace – ever gave the purported stalker a talking to. No, she said, they thought it best to contain the complaint within a controlled group.

She hadn't been happy about it, but she'd agreed to their terms as a peacekeeping measure. 'I felt like I needed to be on good terms with all of them.' The unwritten implication of that was apparent on her face, 'I didn't think I had a choice.'

Her unhappiness had escalated by the end of her first month, however. 'The work atmosphere was so unsavoury. *Sab gaali-galoch karte the. Jhooti kasme khaate the* (People cussed all the time. Swore false oaths. Made vain promises.),' Smita said indignantly. 'I would listen as Karan made lengthy phone calls, swearing on his imaginary children that a client's money would be credited soon. It all felt like a sham.' Smita made up her mind to leave before she was indoctrinated by the herd. The first person she went to speak to, was Deepak. 'I went to his cabin to tell him what I'd decided and somehow, the conversation ended with him giving me his number. He insisted I could trust him and that I should text him if I ever faced any issues in and around the office.'

The messages started pouring in. Thick and fast. I suspect this is when Smita and Deepak's romance began; perhaps her mind always simultaneously remembered during each retelling, what the dalliance led to, because Smita never divulged any sappy details of their time together.

Smita continued, talking very fast and flitting from the end of one syllable to the next, without a pause. When she barrelled through vague phrases that hinted at the beginnings of a relationship, Smita had somehow moved through time.

'They were now making plans to travel to Vaishno Devi.'

'Who?' I asked her.

'Our office couple, Suman and Karan. They said they wanted to make a group and insisted I join in. I wasn't sure but I said I'd ask my parents. *Woh pehli baar maine Deepak ke liye mummy-papa se jhoot bola.* (That was the first time I lied to my parents for Deepak.) I told them it was a college "last hurrah" kind of trip and they both agreed.'

'Around this time, I'd also quit the workplace and interviewed somewhere new in Noida. I remember the date of my interview, 17 December, because that was the day Deepak "proposed [to] me". He sent me a text that said, "I like you". He said, later, that he was too impatient to wait for me to text back and arranged to meet me at the Kashmere Gate terminal. So we did and he sat next to me on a bench, declaring, "*Yaar, main tumhe sach mein like karta hoon.* (I really like you.)" He also told me, flatly, that he wanted no misunderstandings about the warmth of his affections and their extent; he wasn't thinking of marriage, he warned me. I retorted that I hadn't even thought of him that way, so I was alright with only spending time with him. I agreed to us going out on dates.'

Smita hesitated again. Did she do this only at points where she thought she had acceded too soon? Not put her foot down? Given in to her proclivity to please people?

Eventually, as freshly minted boyfriend-and-girlfriend, Deepak and Smita joined the others on a trip to Vaishno Devi that began, she said, on 29 December 2015. The 'others' also included a new couple, Gautam ('I had never seen him before, but he was Deepak's friend') and his girlfriend, Piyali, who, Smita claimed, was married to someone else.

'It was a strange trip. Even before it ... started. At one point, Piyali made me answer her husband's call to tell him we were on an official trip together. Later, I saw cuts slashed across her body and she told me they were courtesy of a series of beatings from Gautam. "Why are you with him if he hits you? And you have a husband," I argued, and she said that she was in love with the man who beat her. "You'll know when you're in love," she told me.'

Years of knowing Smita has made me realize that the situation was more portentous than she thought it could be.

Three rooms had been booked under six names: Deepak and Karan shared one, Suman and Smita, the second, and Gautam and Piyali, the third.

'*Vaishno Devi ka darshan karke jab hum wapas aaye, main kamre mein akeli thi. Us waqt Deepak aaya aur pehli baar mujhse zabardasti karne ki koshish ki.* (When we returned from our trek to Vaishno Devi, I was alone in my room. Just then, Deepak entered my room and for the first time, attempted to molest me.)'

Smita didn't dive into the details, beyond the point that she pushed him off her and horrified, went straight to Karan, who 'I thought of like a brother'. 'Karan asked Deepak to apologize and Deepak threw himself at my feet, clasping his hands and going, "I lost control of my senses, I made a mistake. I'll never do such a thing in my life."'

'What did you say?' I asked her.

'I accepted the half-baked apology,' she said softly. 'And came home and cried in anger and disgust, for days. I'd lied to my mother, so I couldn't tell her what had happened.'

Smita had now started at a new job that paid her a pittance, compared to the toxic call centre she'd left behind – about ₹11,000 a month and conveniences. She had learnt to assure herself that the new circumstances, despite the penury, at least assured her safety. But soon, persistent calls from Karan and Deepak dragged her back into the old cesspool. 'They would call and say, "They're paying you a pittance. Come back here, we'll ensure you are better taken care of. We'll pay you more and we'll make sure the issues you had last time are all ironed out." My resistance weakened and I conceded. I went back to that old place and its poisonous circle of people.'

Once back, she struggled between affection for the man and abhorrence at the crime; she struggled, negotiated and renegotiated with the recollections in the recesses of her memory and, as she later told me, committed the latest incident in that series of developments to their farthest corner.

## IV

'I WASN'T HANGING OUT WITH DEEPAK A LOT ANYMORE, after what had happened in Vaishno Devi. But he didn't like that and he would follow me around. For instance, if I stood up to fill my bottle at the water cooler, or grab my tiffin box from the fridge, he would be right there.'

Unable to summon Smita to be at his beck and call in office, he lashed out harder and faster when they were alone.

Eventually, therefore, the seeds of discord had begun to be sown, and they first manifested as a growing ball of discontent within Smita. Deepak and his coterie, she said, were dissatisfied with the workplace and wanted to leave to establish something of their own.

Yet again, they worked on the pliable and pliant Smita, coaxing the timorous, people-pleasing side out of her, and convinced her to go with them. She followed them on their way out. Free of all managerial control, and therefore, the tight leash that had kept him at bay, Deepak's relationship with his girlfriend turned into a manifestation of all things ugly and sordid.

'Under his direct employ, Deepak started stealing my salary. We would all receive cash payments and in front of the others, he'd pocket my share, saying, "*Tujhse kho jayega, baad mein de dunga.* (You'll lose it, I'll give it to you later.)" When alone, and once I asked for my money, he'd say, "*Yeh humare future ke liye hai, toh mujhe save karne de* (I'm saving this to put it towards our future)."'

Needless to say, Smita didn't see a penny she made. 'I hadn't handed any share of my savings to my parents in two months and had to make up a story about a phone EMI. I even had to borrow daily expenses, like fares for my metro or auto rides, from them, since Deepak would leave me cash-strapped. I felt so humiliated.'

Around this time, her boyfriend had started hitting her like an untrammelled bull. Smita called it 'haath chhorna'. I visibly recoiled at the word. 'I would tell him, "*kis haq se tum mujhpe haath chhod rahe ho*? (Who gives you the right to lay a finger on me?)" I would tell him how much he was making me put up with and yet, despite everything, I was finding it difficult to leave. I'd tell him of my dreams of opening a new institute and how I would, one day, leave all this behind. It may have been just wishful thinking, but he would only get more incensed and scream, "*Kuch zyada bolne nahi lagi hai* (You've started to talk through your hat, haven't you)" and he'd hit me some more.'

Smita stared at us for a moment and we stared back.

'I could never understand him,' she confessed, dazedly attempting to sift through and make sense of the weeks of gratuitous violence that had carved out holes in her insides. The woman I now saw had evidently lost the ability to calibrate right from wrong, at the time, as she continued, 'There was a time when he asked my younger sister to tie him a *rakhi*. A dam broke and I burst out at him, telling him to make up his mind about whether he really wanted me in his life or not, and if not, he should better stay away from my family. I think Deepak was gradually beginning to realize that I was getting disillusioned with him.'

Whether it was the actual fear of her disenchantment or the pique to his ego, Smita didn't know, but nothing could have informed her of what he was about to do. I've often suspected she left out the far more sordid, far more darker details while telling me her story; perhaps, stories of more beatings, followed by threats of her walking out? Perhaps, there were anecdotes of her expressing a wish to be independent of him, of finally doing things other than to 'keep the peace'. I couldn't know if Smita had omitted these, but what she did spell out, were the subsequent weeks of absolute malevolence.

'I was sick, one day and didn't go to office. Karan called at my house several times and my mom told him about my fever. I think he was calling on behalf of

Deepak, who had too much of an ego to call me himself. Then, Deepak called me and said something that chilled me to the bone. He demanded that I meet him, and when I pleaded a fever, he said, "*Mujhe kuch nahi pata. Tu abhi Kashmere Gate aayegi. Nahi to Suman ne teri kuch aisi pic le rakhi hai jo main leak karwa dunga.* (I'm not going to stand for your defiance. You're going to come to Kashmere Gate right away. If you don't, well, Suman has a few photographs of you that I'll have no qualms in 'leaking' to the world.)'"

'I felt like the ground beneath my feet had shifted. Suman was my friend and she'd stayed over at my place, many nights,' at this point, Smita looked up at me, as though emphasizing a point, 'Women fool around in front of each other all the time, but I had no idea she had taken untoward photos of me, without my knowledge. How could she have violated my trust like that?'

Smita found herself dragging her feet to Kashmere Gate and from there, accompanying her blackmailer to his house.

'Deepak opened the door to his house and let me in. *Usi ke ghar pe usne mera rape kiya. Main bahut cheekhi. Uske padosiyo ne shayad dhyan nahi diya ... Bahut haatha-payi bhi hui.* (He raped me in his own home. I shouted over and over. Perhaps, his neighbours didn't hear me ... I wrestled him for a long, long time.)'

Smita's voice was beginning to whittle down to a series of tinny, breathless sounds. She had stopped racing furiously from the end of one syllable to the next, and had now paused longer than she had during the entire hour-long conversation. She made a quick, wordless gesture towards certain body parts, before saying, 'He left marks on my body; they're still there. I couldn't ward him off of me.'

Much later, I would attempt to change the way she described her rape; the language she unconsciously applied to herself as an object, as a mere receptacle of all things monstrous and vile. Phrases such as 'shame' and 'guilt' and a sense of 'deserving what was coming' floated about her being, and had become so horrifically entrenched in her by then that it was hard to dissociate *her* from the adumbrations she had created of herself – a person whom things were done to. A person without selfhood.

For months and in fact, years after the incident, she would reframe and reshape her narrative in her head – and to me – to suit that idea of herself.

But Smita's story was far from over.

'*Usne yeh sab to kiya, par pata nahi kab usne camera on kar diya tha.* (In the midst of all this, he had switched on a camera, I don't know when.) It must have been kept somewhere near the bed. I don't know when it all happened ... but while he went at me, that camera filmed shots of me. I was too scared to go home. I walked about for a while. I called Karan and told him what had happened in a numbed voice. I couldn't tell you what I was feeling. I eventually walked home at some point, I don't even remember when, and cried so long and so loudly that my mother began to knock on my door worriedly. *Kuch nahi bataya unhe* (I didn't tell her anything). I also stopped going to work for the next couple of days; my mother thought it was because of my fever. All that time, as I sat at home, I was petrified; petrified that he would go ahead and upload those pictures he had said Suman had of me. He was still siphoning off my salary. When I saw him after a few days, he said something random like, "*Mujhse rishta rakhna* ... (Keep your ties with me ...)" And I could only tell him that now that he had gotten what he had wanted, how did it matter?'

Yet, abject fragments of what once was and what could have been, had remained lodged – it was apparent – in Smita's head. She couldn't and didn't file a police complaint for rape. She couldn't and didn't tell a person of authority or a friend or family member, who could have helped in registering said complaint against a man who had perpetrated a crime. She *couldn't* and *didn't* – whether upon instruction or otherwise – cut off her ties with him and instead, remained in that perpetual state of uneasy, miserable longing that had plagued her for the better part of the year, since she'd known this man.

# V

THINGS ESCALATED QUICKLY.

'It was after a workday. The "group" as it were, had walked out together and the men decided to bait me to get a rise out of me. One of them casually mentioned that Deepak's family was going to be visiting families of prospective brides, soon, to "find a girl" for him. I was speechless. I lashed out at Deepak's sister who I was friends with and told her, "Your brother has ruined my life. He raped me, got a friend to take photographs of me and now he's going to waltz off and get married?'"

I must have visibly winced as Smita enunciated her supposed ruination, because she smiled as I shook my head. It would be years, however, until she got to the point where she no longer reverted to her old linguistic fallbacks – the language of 'shame' used to cut oneself down to an insignificant size.

But Smita had digressed; she promptly returned to the conversation between the men in the group and her, 'You could say I'd finally had it. I had lost every semblance of control and now suddenly, I burst out at each one of them, in turn. I told the men that they'd rue the day they thought I was weak. I told Suman I wouldn't wish a friend like her on my worst enemy – how could she have shared photos of me with these men? I just started screaming on the streets and declaring, almost to no one in particular, that Deepak wasn't going to look at prospective brides, if I could help it.'

No such eventuality ever actually took place, Smita claimed, but her colleagues gradually decimated every shred of friendship they'd shown unto her, before. Deepak, too, after all the insouciant references to their 'romance' – perhaps in the hopes of thwarting her ideas of going to the police – in the days right after he had assaulted her, pulled away.

'I remember that it was 13 March 2016, when I went to his place for the last time. I used to tutor his little sister. She had her computer open with his Facebook profile showing and I could tell that he had a new girlfriend. When he was dropping me home, I asked him about it and he just offhandedly said that he'd *always* had another girlfriend, and I had another crying fit. We were almost at my place, and my parents, who, by now, had come to know about the relationship (but not about the rape), intervened.'

But he told them, unceremoniously, '*Isi ne galat samjha. Maine to hamesha sirf dost samjha tha.* (She misunderstood. I've always only thought of Smita as a friend.)'

'I thought that was it. That I'd never see him again. Three months flew by like a whirlwind before I heard from him. I'd just joined a new workplace and I had uploaded photos of myself – happy, all smiles, wearing makeup and new clothes. He texted me, out of the blue, on 10 May, I remember, and wrote, "*Ye kaisi pics daal rakhi hai tune? Inko delete kar.* (What are these pictures you've uploaded? Delete them.)" I wrote back, demanding to know why. He said that I should have worn a jacket; should have covered myself up. My rage came to the fore and I told him in no uncertain terms that he should mind his own business. And then, came the dreaded rejoinder, "*Main tujhse milna chahta hoon* (I want to meet you.) Tell people that you have a meeting for work and you must go. If you don't, I'm sure you remember the pictures."'

'I was petrified all over again. I thought we were past this – hadn't he said he was happy with someone else? I thought *I* was past this – hadn't I left my fear and paranoia behind, three months ago? But once again, that familiar sinking feeling of dread stole over me, and once again, I felt powerless to do anything about him. I resisted the urge to respond to his calls for two days and on the night of 11 May – I still remember the time – it was 11:55 p.m. – he uploaded a couple of photographs from the library of photos that Suman had clicked of me. I had to coax, cajole and wheedle him into deleting those. That was it. I no longer had a choice.'

'On the night of 12 May, I told my mother I had a meeting to attend with Deepak. They objected vociferously because they remembered the end of that relationship unfold right in front of their eyes, but somehow, I convinced them.

'When I went to the hotel that Deepak had told me about on the phone, I found that it had curiously been booked under my name and only mine. I went up to the room to find him waiting for me, bottles of beer and a packet of cigarettes casually strewn on the carpet, as though together, they had formed an ambush.'

Smita looked over at us in anguish. 'I didn't think that – you know, *anything* could happen. I was on my period, so all the way there, I'd thought, "I'm safe. I just need to get him to delete those photos but otherwise, he won't try a thing. I'm safe."'

I spent many gut-wrenching moments afterwards, as I compiled the stories of Meera and Ranjini months

later, thinking about how all these women had assumed
a menstrual cycle would lend them immunity from
an assault that they otherwise had almost certainly
expected. I thought of how they believed that a bodily
function treated with absolute repugnance by most
cisgender heterosexual men, would evidently stump
a man who was about to commit rape. I thought,
therefore, of how their rapes proved the exact opposite
– baffling centuries of our most carefully guarded rape
apologia – that only women who dress, breathe, smell
and act a certain way are raped; the rest, the precious
few, the 'others', are spared.

To this day, nothing has shaken me more than the
words Smita used to describe what happened after, in
the room she was summoned to. The sheer retelling of
the feral rage of the act seemed to gouge out my insides.

'He came at me like a dog throws itself at meat,'
she explained. 'I didn't know what he intended to do
exactly, even as I entered the room. As I watched, he
popped a pill – I read the label on the bottle and it
said "Kamasutra". I started to shout. I don't think it
mattered. He didn't care about that. He didn't care that
I was on my period, he didn't care about anything – he
just tore at me, over and over again. I remember that my
father called, sometime in the middle and I tried to grab
my phone, but he snatched it away and threw it to the
floor. He did things to me that were bestial. The memory
of it gives me goosebumps.'

Smita stopped to caress a goose-pimpled forearm,
crying the whole time. She wasn't done. 'I felt limp, like

I had no power in me to do anything after a point. I'd frozen and given up. Even as I lay there, he splashed beer from one of the bottles on the folds of my salwar so that later, it would look like I'd been drinking with him. He lit a cigarette and forced it between my lips to make it seem like I'd been smoking.

'There was no act of diabolism he hadn't thought of. My body had been ...'

Here, she gave up. In the midst of the wordless silence, three people cried. Smita, the loudest, face partially concealed behind the crease of her collared shirt. My colleague, into his camera, as he started to walk off. I'd proceeded, blurry-eyed, towards Smita, but a woman with the organizing party, who'd walked out of the congregation at the time, got there first.

Smita sobbed into her shoulder.

## VI

I NEVER USED THE VIDEO CLIP OF THAT INTERVIEW.

Smita had not asked me not to, neither did she reach out at any point in the weeks after to tell me she'd rather that I didn't.

But I didn't feel up to it. I had spent the minutes after Smita had broken down, staring at the lines of ink on her face and muttering inanities about the texture of her kohl and the colour of her stole. She'd grinned weakly and graciously offered a line in return, eventually ending our strange, heady, heavy encounter with a bartering of phone numbers and email addresses. That muggy

December morning may have been my first brush with a story that wasn't cold. A story with wounds that were still open and festering and that hurt to the touch.

I hadn't met anyone like Smita, hitherto, whose naive geniality – especially in the light of what I'd heard – both exasperated me and filled me with wonder.

I reached out to her, a couple of months later, in early 2017, for no apparent reason and with no story in sight. She couldn't recognize me off the bat, when I mentioned I was a reporter who had once interviewed her. She hazarded a couple of erroneous guesses at names of women, before I interjected with a 'We were both crying at the end, do you remember?'

'Yes, of course!' she exclaimed and we laughed in unison. We decided to meet at a nondescript CCD behind a ramshackle building in a north Delhi colony, a part of town that I had never been to before. But I was quickly going to realize that a friendship with Smita meant acceding to specific physical parameters and geographical off-limits, born from equal parts self-preservation and paranoia.

I can't recall exactly how our conversations flowed from one meeting to another, but they seemed to find their own ebb and flow – short, halting conversations coalescing into one wholesome friendship. Most conversations – after circuiting the ambit of work talk, new friends she'd made, how her parents were Bengali like mine, but how unlike mine, had not been able to impart the language to her – we'd drift off into the uneasy certainties.

'Do you think he'll ever be punished?'

'Do you want him to be punished?' I asked her searchingly, trying to look into her clouded gaze.

It was hard to tell with Smita. Some days she was bitter, acrid, even. One afternoon, on a cold coffee date that she'd come late to, she explained herself acrimoniously, '*Us Deepak ke wajah se kuch sahi nahi raha.* (Nothing is the same anymore because of that Deepak.)' Do you know I have a wound on my left breast that I just went to the doctor about, for the nth time? He had bit me so hard in that hotel room and because I did nothing about it for weeks, the wound developed sepsis. It hurt like crazy for months. Sometimes, it still does. Today, I grazed my scar against the end of my dresser and it began to bleed.' She cried like she often did, albeit this time, more in anger than in remorse.

On other days, she'd sit looking wistfully into the distance. Sometimes, bizarrely, when a couple walked into the cafe holding hands, she'd pipe up, 'Deepak and I would hold hands, too. He'd insist, even on office premises.'

When we spoke about love, in general, or about relationships of people we knew, in particular, she found a meandering way to slip in his references, often voluntarily, oftener involuntarily. When we discussed the fate of her 'case' in its strictest legalese, she chose to condemn him with the choicest imprecations, often angry, oftener heartbroken.

Once, when we met at a cafe very near her new workplace, she swooped down upon me with glee writ large on her face. 'Did you hear? A man who raped a seven-year-old girl in this neighbourhood has been arrested. He had fled, but they tracked him down and put him in jail. I hope he gets punished!' Her professed happiness was augmented by an unstoppable rush of adrenaline, even as her fists clenched into balls by her hips. For a while, I couldn't get her to talk of anything else.

Another time, she called to ask if she could 'Facebook messenger' me a flurry of strange texts she had received from an unknown number. 'They're all hi's and hello's, but no one responds when I ask "Who's this?"' she said in a conspiratorial whisper. I could tell that her mind had drifted hopelessly and immediately to only one suspect, but neither of us pressed the point.

Funnily, I've browsed through Smita's messages at her behest, a good dozen times, over the last couple of years, and they've all been under instruction to sift through reams of saucy texts from unsaved phone numbers; all in order to figure out their 'mysterious sender'. The question in her eyes never changes; it is always the same question, but it is never asked aloud.

We got to talking about the interview we had filmed and that had cemented our friendship; Smita insisted that she'd like to do it all over again. 'I'd like to tell my story, but the story of what happened to him next. *How* I got justice. And won.' To tell that story, I reminded her, she'd have to truly pursue her case, instead of allowing it to run threadbare into cold waters at intermittent intervals. She'd have to pick it up and run with it, I emphasized.

Smita vouched for wanting nothing more and so, we set about meeting for interviews in earnest to supplement the story she'd already told me, eventually creating the chassis for this book.

I had reason enough to insist on her persistence; to stoke the slightest ember of a fire in her, any time it reared its head. For Smita, by her own admission, had told no one about her rape for days after it happened. She'd goaded herself into silence, the first time, and by the second, assured herself of the futility of police involvement.

'For a week after that night in the hotel room, I shut myself up completely,' she told me, by the time our third meeting rolled around. 'I would hide the bruises, clothe my scars under dupattas and just cry ceaselessly, both in physical torment and sheer disbelief. I couldn't believe I had let it happen to me again! If I couldn't believe myself, would my parents? I thought if I tell them, they'll also smell the beer; catch a whiff of the cigarettes – the beer I never drank and the cigarettes I never smoked. They'll think I brought this on myself, and so will the rest of the world. So I cried and I cried, and I kept mum.'

Months later, I was told by Kranti Khode, Sangeeta Parmar and a team of women coordinators at Jan Sahas, who eventually counselled her, that she'd tried to take her own life. Smita had pointed out stray scars on her forearm much, much after – it was hard to discern one scar from the other in a patch of skin riddled by deep, squiggly lines, both from her assault and from the self-infliction that followed.

She'd described, once or twice, the depths of the darkness she'd found herself in, during that long, long week post 12 May – indeed, that whole year leading up to it, after she'd met Deepak. But we've never dwelt on it and I take solace in the fact that she found the waiting ears and the ready arms of her family and friends, not long after.

It began with one phone call. Disconcerted by her own ennui, Smita had started to scour possible sources on the internet for help. On 17 May 2016, she discovered an ad for a rape survivors' helpline after a quick Google search, and called the number.

'The first time I made that call, I didn't know what to say. How do you just blurt out the truth to a perfunctory voice over the telephone?'

Smita burst into tears at the first 'hello' and eventually managed to relay her truth that she'd been raped. And that she wanted help.

There were a bunch of follow-up calls from the NGO, which connected her to one of its Delhi-based executives, Ruby. This Ruby promised to accompany her to the police station and promised not to leave, and so, that was where Smita finally headed to, on 19 May – seven days after her rape.

## VII

THE 'COLD CASE' OF SMITA'S RAPE GETS CURIOUSER AND curiouser by the day.

For one, her first court summons appeared in November 2018 – exactly two and a half years after her

FIR had been registered. Why did it take so long? What justified the agonizing wait of two years, for even the semblance of a judicial process to begin?

For another, the summons would never have appeared – by law of natural progression – if her FIR had not been registered.

And it very nearly wasn't.

When Smita landed up at Jaitpur Police Station in southeast Delhi on 19 May 2016, she was told exactly what she'd feared she would be: that she was never raped at all, and that she was only fabricating her assault in an attempt to resuscitate a dead relationship.

'For the longest time, the cops – after they'd heard my story – refused to file an FIR. They wouldn't even listen after a point and began to laugh in my face,' she recalled. 'One of them said, "Boyfriend *tha, na? Pyaar ka chakkar tha. Do saal toh ghoomi ho uske saath. Toh ab kyun bhadak rahi ho?* (He was your boyfriend, wasn't he? You were in a relationship. You also hung out with him of your own free will, for two years. So why are you lashing out now?)"

In vain did Smita lift coat sleeves and part the buttons on her blouse to display signs of her 'own free will'. Until Ruby stepped in, there were no takers for Smita's story, her voice, or in fact, the lacerations on her skin.

'It was troubling,' Sangeeta, who I'd first met when we'd gone to interview Ranjini, and who was now Smita's case worker, told me. 'There was complete disregard for an allegation of rape that had happened not once, but twice.'

Hours of wheedling, coaxing and browbeating ultimately persuaded the crop of policemen at Jaitpur Police Station to write up an FIR. To this day, it is one of the most carelessly written, inattentive police reports I have ever read; and I have reread and scrutinized the part-Hindi, part-English report in sheer disbelief many a times, attempting to make some sense of it.

For one, the FIR is poorly written – not merely in terms of the handwriting, which is illegible, or the grammar and syntax or the lack thereof – but also in terms of the abysmal summary of the case. For another, the report jumps from one timeframe in Smita's narrative, to another, without making any attempt to connect the dots. It also appears to blur the lines between legitimate police language and what could easily be mistaken for a cautionary tale. For example, while it takes a precious amount of time setting up Smita's love story with Deepak, choosing to embellish it with phrases like '*Dono mein aana jana hua aur pyaar hua* (The two started to hang out and there developed a romance),' the account of her first rape is filtered through sentences like 'The accused had promised the victim of (sic) marriage and engaged in a sexual relationship with the victim ...'

But where are the larger, more vivid, flagrant details of rape? Why is the first occurrence misrepresented as 'engaging in sexual relations'? Where is the pertinent mention of a superior at work sexually harassing a subordinate? The FIR distractedly picks up little details of their relationship – like how the accused would withhold the complainant's salary – and yet, writes no details about how she had been raped by her colleague, whom she had, to quote the travesty verbatim, 'Known for the past two years'.

Why the insistence on setting up her story like a love affair gone wrong? Why the inexplicable bias towards an accused who hadn't even testified, while colouring, editing and screening the words of the woman in front of them, which they were supposed to put on paper?

Ruby and the rest of Jan Sahas found it hard to follow up with the IO on Smita's case for a long time after. 'We were completely rebuffed and we didn't feel like we were getting all the cooperation we could have,' Sangeeta told me over the phone and Smita reiterated, 'I would call the station a lot, at first, because I had hope. I would hope that they'd investigate Deepak, arrest him for his crime, but every time I asked, they sounded dismissive. When I went there a second time with my father, they laughed in my face.'

The company of her father, though, had meant the world to Smita. 'I didn't tell them for the longest time,' she told me once, as we argued the necessity of her extending her social circumference to beyond her home. In response to my entreaties, Smita had tried to deconstruct her two-year journey with her parents. 'The NGO encouraged me to tell them; they said I needed their support once the fight got harder. So I told them, a week after filing the FIR.'

Her parents were horrified, but not for the reasons Smita had feared they would be. They had known her alleged rapist, met the man, befriended him, thought of him as their daughter's future husband – because that is what Smita and Deepak had conditioned them, over time, into naturally believing. Yet, just months into knowing Smita, I could tell that while she believed – somewhere in the darkest, dankest, most fearful recesses of her memory – that her parents *blamed* her for her own rape, they, in fact, only lamented the loss of her selfhood. This was obvious to the naked eye – any eye that wasn't Smita's. Her mind offered no easy alternatives; no respite from the punishment she continued to inflict on herself, believing that this chapter was entirely something she'd invited upon herself.

How do I know this? Because several cold coffee soirees (our usual poison of choice) were punctuated by my persistently hissing, 'You know it isn't your fault, right? *None* of it is.' The fact was obvious; as obvious as the noses on our faces. Yet, every one of those times, Smita would respond with a 'Then why do I feel like it is?' and smile the smile of someone resigned to their self-deprecation.

Yet, wondrous, marvellous little changes started to make their appearance in Smita's psyche, over time. They appeared like crests and troughs in our own friendship; from being unwilling to hang out near Kashmere Gate terminal around the one-year mark since her rape, Smita would now suggest going to a local market near the metro station, only months ago, for us to pick up cheap winter scarves. From loathing the idea of alcohol and cigarettes as contraband that had been slathered on her body against her will like markers of her rape,

Smita went to a local watering hole with a couple of colleagues in early 2018. 'I tried a breezer and found it not so bitter,' she made a face and then laughed. 'Of course, I didn't tell anyone at home.' Just the fact that the idea of alcohol acting as an accomplice in her rape had dissipated and become something mischievous and truant, filled me with glee. I could tell Smita treated it like a watershed moment, too.

Several other such moments ensued. Like her joining a gym, back in June 2017. 'I can lift more than some of the new guys can,' she boasted one day. 'My trainer is really proud of me.' This woman with a renewed sense of her own physical strength stood before me in stark contrast to the woman who'd described her own 'helplessness', only a year ago.

Then, there was the time she finally started to talk of male friends who'd expressed a romantic interest in her. Was she interested in turn? She didn't know, she admitted. 'I loved once and it ended horribly,' she mused, facing the blackhole of her despair again, ready to disappear into it at the slightest provocation.

The blackhole still turns up. It turns up in the form of sappy WhatsApp statuses and Facebook posts that betray the ambiguity of her mind. Smita and I have often lost touch with one another for lengthy periods of time, over the years. At such times, I know Smita will reach out when she wants to; when she'd like to talk. At such times, her social media is a landmine of information. Sepia-toned stock silhouettes of women in tears, couples with their backs to one another, a metaphorical setting sun inundate her Facebook timeline – often accompanied by saccharine captions to the tune of 'love is lost'. To the lay observer, these are the ramblings of a hopeless romantic. To the one who knows Smita, these are products of an extremely troubled mind – one that remembers both the love and the crime, and hates herself for it.

## VIII

I LOST TOUCH WITH SMITA, SOMETIME IN THE MIDDLE of 2018. Our friendship was so heavily skewed towards her making the first move – picking up the phone to tell me about her feelings – that when I didn't hear from her in days, I assumed she was fine.

The days turned into weeks and eventually, months. When I finally did pick up the phone guiltily, after almost three months of going incommunicado, I found that her number no longer existed.

In panic, I reached out to counsellors at the NGO, who I assumed were still handling her case, and was told that she'd changed her number because she'd gotten married, and before being offered her new one. When I finally got through to her, she sounded simultaneously delighted to hear from me and profusely apologetic for not having kept in touch: she'd severed ties with her past when she'd been arranged-married, and now, was on the brink of divorce.

Smita claimed that her husband had beaten her, verbally abused her and cheated on her, in the course of the three months that they'd been married. 'Bad things keep happening to me,' she said succinctly of the situation, in the near-resigned, almost-defeated tone I'd become unused to hearing.

We seemed to be making up for lost time. There were so many questions. Why had she gotten married? She'd capitulated when her parents insisted. She'd cried at the wedding. She'd cried after. They'd withheld all information of her rape from his family. He'd never understood her. She'd felt lonelier and more miserable than she had in months.

She'd returned. As of November 2018, they were divorcing. Little snippets of information encapsulated this chapter of Smita's story.

Her parents had dictated – and she had internalized, as she admitted in the only meeting we had, a few days before her divorce – that marrying would equal forgetting. That the narrative of rape that defined her would be shed like old skin and she'd rise like a phoenix from the ashes.

She told me, during our brief tête-à-tête days before her divorce, that she thought that sex was a terrible thing. '*Ganda*' (awful) was the word she used. 'Maybe, one day, with someone you love, with someone who loves you?' I had hedged, but Smita had left behind such stargazing romanticisms, by then, viewing her body as merely a canvas for scoring victories and losses by the men she'd loved and lost. She looked at her body, by then, as something that bore the physical and figurative spoils of the wars that had been wrought on it, and her heart, with the steely indifference of someone who could no longer be won over. Strangely, I could tell she thought of herself as *separate* from her body. 'I do not think of sex as love. I can only equate it to violence,' she had said tonelessly.

A couple of conversations after this rather tragic meeting, told me that there still existed, within Smita's psyche, the old crests and troughs that were so typical of her. The tug-of-war between *her* love and *his* crime, between fighting and forgetting.

After months of willing herself to forget, she was now choosing to fight.

Smita's first court summons appeared in November 2018 – the same month she filed for divorce, and over a year and a half since she had filed her FIR. She faced a courtroom in Saket District Court in December and said what she had to say, screaming out her testimony; crying, at times. Sangeeta, her case worker, filled me in, 'Smita had once again subsided into periods of long silences and deliberate brevity, when speaking about her case – choosing not to, at many points. Her next hearing is a few months from now,' Sangeeta told me.

So I spoke to her a few months from then. In April 2019, to be precise. The trial was well underway and there had been five hearings up to that point. She was pleased with the magistrate, she said, and horrified by the attorney defending the man she's accused of rape – or more precisely, by his interrogation. 'I cannot believe what they have been asking me, during the cross [examination]. Deepak's lawyer spent the last hearing talking about how I smoke and drink, and how the judge must decry the statements that come out from the mouth of a woman like that. But the judge intervenes on my behalf – she rebukes the opposing team for saying anything offensive or insulting to me.' She'd had a similar encouraging experience with the judicial magistrate, she said, who'd recorded her statement under section 164 of the CrPC (whereby 'any Metropolitan Magistrate or Judicial Magistrate may, whether or not he has jurisdiction in the case, record any confession or statement made to him ... at any time ... before the commencement of the inquiry or trial').[1]

In September 2017, a two-judge bench of the Punjab and Haryana High Court awarded bail to three law students who had previously been convicted by a lower court for gang-raping a woman student. In its bail order, the court called the woman 'promiscuous' and complained that 'her narrative does not throw up gut-wrenching violence that normally precede or accompany such incidents ... The testimony of the victim does offer an alternate story of casual relationship with her friends, acquaintances, adventurism and experimentation in sexual encounters and these factors would, therefore, offer compelling reasons to consider the prayer for suspension of sentence.'[2]

How could this have happened in that case – and in multiple other documented instances of character assassination in courts – when, in 2002, character assassination was specifically prohibited through an amendment in the Indian Evidence (Amendment) Act, 2002. 'It shall not be permissible to put questions in the cross-examination of the prosecutrix as to her general immoral character.'[3]

The groundbreaking amendments of the 2013 Criminal Law (Amendment) Act – after Nirbhaya – also sought to put an end to the double victimization survivors face (through harassment in court). But it has clearly not filtered down to courts across the country, including Smita's.

The Smita I spoke to in the early months of 2019 wasn't timorous about a fight anymore; she'd cry intermittently, then subsequently declare she was stronger than she'd ever been. Was she ambivalent, still, about her feelings? She wasn't, she said. I offered to accompany her to the next hearing if she'd have me and she professed her gladness at the proposal, 'I've asked my parents not to come after they did to the first two hearings. I don't want to subject them to the defence's acerbic cross-examination of me. It has just been my lawyer and I since.'

Sadly, our conferences – true to recent form – vacillated over the year, from intense hour-long phone marathons to periods of emptiness where we heard nothing from each other. Smita hibernated for months and I stayed true to the yo-yo-ing nature of our relationship, by trying not to interfere, confident that she'd be back. After months of not answering calls, her number went dead and I was worried. Again.

I shouldn't have been. In April 2020, Smita reached out with alacrity, saying she'd changed her number, as though nothing else had changed.

Yet, so much had. She had married again, for one. She had tired of her trial, for another. 'The last time I went to a hearing was in August 2019. Since then, I've asked my lawyer not to involve me until it's over. *Isko khatam karke do bas, maine bola.*' (Finish it for me, I told her.)

Did it matter if she won? Did it matter if she lost?

Negative.

'I don't care anymore,' she said flatly. 'That chapter's given me nothing but grief. I don't want the past to overshadow what I have today.' She explained her recalcitrance away with a 'the trial came to me at a point when I had already moved on; had started to put the pieces of me back together again', but she needn't have. Her recalcitrance can be traced unassumingly across the four years of being raped (by her rapist), being disbelieved (by the police), being policed (by herself) and being patient (for a trial that never begun). When the law finally came knocking on Smita's door, she had reduced herself to rubble that could no longer be reassembled.

Tired of no one championing her cause, Smita had given up.

At a point like that – and some months after the actualization of her divorce – Smita met her now-husband. Her voice lit up when she mentioned him, 'he was introduced to me through common family friends.

We got married on 11 December. I'm lucky to have a man like him – to have finally found peace.'

The peace is a delicately engineered one, that Smita guards with desperation – she has not told him about her rape. 'I can never tell him,' she said immediately, when asked. 'He knows I was married before and was extremely understanding of the circumstances that that man put me through. I cannot imagine how he will react if he knows about this.'

But the knowledge had been harder and harder for her to safeguard – ever since she had faced the man she had accused of raping her, at the last hearing she went to, in August 2019. Suddenly, Smita's voice changed to the timbre low and frightened. 'I met him in the hallway outside the courtroom – Deepak and his father – and I lost it. I don't know what came over me, but I just saw his eyes – dead, cold, remorseless – and I had flashbacks of every horrible thing he'd done to me. I remember walking inside in a daze, barely able to see three feet ahead of me. Halfway across, I fainted.'

Smita was rushed to Mahavir Hospital in Saket – close to the district court – and there, heard doctors tell her mother she was not to be under any duress, or her emotional equilibrium would be in serious jeopardy. She was weakened, she was told, every time she thought of the past, every time she saw the man who raped her. 'The doctors looked at my reports from when I had first gotten my 'medical' (MLC, subsequent to her FIR claiming rape) done and received counselling, and ascertained that I had been given anti-depressants. Those medicines had helped, they said, and would help again, and they prescribed me a daily dosage. They also told me I needed to get psychiatric help again, in order to ensure I didn't hurt anymore. They were actually really kind.'

She forgets now, she said. Little things. Minor details. She didn't know if it was the medicine or 'my own mind; but I feel blank sometimes, misplacing objects, skipping chores. I think it has to do with my seeing *him*. Ever since I saw him, I have been gripped by this terror – I don't know of what, but it's palpable.'

She didn't remember details of her rape anymore very assiduously, she said, but they came to her when she least expected it, in her dreams. 'There are nights when I dream of that hotel room and what happened inside it, and I wake up with a start. My husband started to keep a glass of water on the bedside table for me when he began to notice this. He doesn't know what my nightmares are.'

Just the night before, she said, she had tossed and turned in bed till 4 a.m. 'He tried to talk to me and I was so overwhelmed by the delirium, I turned my back to him. My husband lost his temper like he never had before and said that if I didn't behave myself, he'd fling my phone across the room. That did it.'

The tirade had snapped Smita out of her reverie – or rather, pushed her into the sordidness of her subconscious, where inhabited Deepak and memories of his gratuitous violence. 'He would speak to me that way – send direct insults and slaps my way if I wasn't "behaving properly". He would throw my phone away, too, if I tried to call someone for help.'

The horrific resemblance to her husband's words, that night, broke her. She crumpled to a heap by the bed and sat there in a trance, resting her head against the bedstead. Finally, finding his wife immune to his entreaties, her husband had called his wife's mother. 'She asked me quietly if it had anything to do with Deepak and I told her "yes". She then asked me to remember what the doctors had said and to calm myself. The worst part was, even in all this, my husband still doesn't know why I get that way.'

The uncertainties creep up on her in the stealth of the night, when she least expects it; often, it is when he attempts to romance her. Oftener, it is when he attempts to draw her closer and slither a hand across her body. 'I slap it away,' she said expectantly. Yet, 'he's always been gentle. Never left a bruise or a mark on my skin.' Smita's instincts for self-preservation have wildly deluded her notions of what the parameters of sex can be and how far they can be pushed. To her, the absence of a bruise on her already scarred flesh is a sign that she should be grateful.

We speak primarily of that instinct for sexual safety, therefore, and how she can navigate around it, to a space where she can make love to her husband without fear. I don't know if we reach it at the end of our phone call, but we strategize with warmth and laughter – our old laughter – and threw up 'trauma therapy' as a good starting point for her.

Does Smita's story end on a note of hope? Perhaps.

Perhaps, I've regained our conferences, too. Perhaps she *is* stronger now: no longer prone to subjecting herself to the systemic self-decimation and self-deprecation, as she has, for so long. Perhaps, before all this is over, she will have reconciled to the four-year-long tug-of-war in her head – between fighting (a rapist) and forgetting (the rape). Perhaps, she will have negotiated a middle ground, where, after shedding the baggage of a rape, a trial or a marriage, she can finally be free.

## An Epilogue

I feel like Smita's story deserves an epilogue because of the many questions it asks but doesn't answer. The biggest one being: how did so many travesties happen right under people's noses without anyone offering any resistance?

Before her own transfiguration into and self-representation as a rape survivor; before her marriage and its abuse; before her second marriage and its trepidations, Smita was once a mere employee. And as an employee, she should have been protected by a Prevention of Sexual Harassment at Work (PoSH) Act, instituted in 2013 – a long time before she entered the workforce.

**Offence #1:** Long before Deepak ever began a relationship with her, an office boy – Smita has claimed – would idle by her cubicle. He would stalk her as she left office to go home, she has alleged. She has also alleged that she told a senior employee, Karan, about the boy and the alleged stalking, and yet, her team lead chose to dawdle on (and dismiss) the complaint, rather than forwarding it to an Internal Complaints Committee (ICC), as mandated by the PoSH Act. Did Smita's old workplace even have an ICC? Had it formed one within the several months that Smita worked there? It is doubtful, since, when asked, she doesn't mention a single female mentor whom she could have approached. She doesn't mention awareness programmes, orientations or workshops conducted to gender-sensitize an almost entirely male team, which should, by rights, have been legally protecting the minority, anyway. Neither does she recollect ever being given a primer on an existing ICC at the company that she could approach, if she was ever sexually harassed during her time there, *as she was.*

The PoSH Act clearly states that any company with ten or more employees needs to constitute an ICC by an order of the employer in writing. However, even *this* numerical threshold isn't set in stone, 'At the district level, the Government is required to set up a "local committee" (LC) to investigate and redress complaints of sexual harassment from the unorganized sector or from establishments where the IC has not been constituted on account of the establishment having less than ten employees or if the complaint is against the employer.'[4] The fine print of what is actually quite an assiduously written law can be read at the link I have cited – *or* if you pick up the manual which your company should have in digital or print form. If not, you might want to ask the pertinent question, along with another one: has the employer obeyed the provision to constitute an ICC? Because if not, he/she/they would be liable for a monetary penalty under law, in case a complaint is made to the magistrate. In fact, repeated non-compliance can even result in de-registration of the business or revocation of any business licenses that were granted by the government or local authority.

If Smita had *known* of this violation – known that her workplace had wilfully flouted a pretty tough-as-nails Act, specific to her specific problem – could she have filed an FIR more airtight than the one she ultimately did, for her rape? She didn't know, and overtly, it should have been the job of the police team who registered her FIR, to have done so under the sections of that Act, rather than just the IPC. For, very much like the POCSO, Acts that are idiosyncratic, Acts that have individual character and Acts that were built to serve a narrow scope – historically – afford better protection and legal success than the all-encompassing IPC.

Why did her IO not have the acumen to arm her with this?

**Offence #2:** The most arrant offence – within the purview of the PoSHA – was, of course, committed when Deepak, fully armed with the paraphernalia and wherewithal to sexually abuse a subordinate, went on to do so. Like a panther stalking its prey, the man circled her for days, even releasing commissaries to do his bidding – like when a colleague guilefully suggested that she enlist the help of the man who would go on to rape her, to get rid of the man who had been stalking her.

Here is a place where the state could have done better by her. Its interjections – ensuring that all workplaces have ICCs, that their founders and managers sensitize employees about ICCs, that employees *know* they're safe – would have infused in Smita, a stronger sense of self, thereby according her the will to fight.

Smita represents the sum total of the state's failure to deliver justice – a justice promised nearly twenty years ago.

Her story – if 'her' is every woman like her, who has been raped by somebody at work and repudiated – begins not in 2018, but in 1992.

Now, it was as recently as 2013, that the government of India revamped corporate governance through the groundbreaking PoSHA. The victory of 2013, however, was the light at the end of a very long, very long-winded tunnel – for one woman, in particular. When Bhanwari Devi, a Dalit woman, was gang-raped in 1992 while discharging her duties as a social worker and attempting to stop a child marriage in Bhateri, Rajasthan,[5] the uproar against feudal patriarchy was spearheaded by one welfare group, Vishaka. Vishaka's petition to introduce a law to protect women like Bhanwari Devi, made it to the Supreme Court.

It was during *Vishaka vs State of Rajasthan* in 1997, that the Supreme Court of India observed that 'equality in employment can be seriously impaired if women are subjected to gender-specific violence, such as sexual harassment in the workplace'.[6] On the heels of the Supreme Court's landmark ruling, therefore, came the Vishaka Guidelines, following which, employers across India would have to set up safer work spaces for women. Importantly, prior to Vishaka, women who were assaulted or harassed at the office, could only register FIRs under the IPC (Sections 354 and 509) – something that Smita was compelled to do in 2018.

Each company then, from 1997, began to set up 'Vishaka Committees' to ensure the guidelines were followed, until 2007, when the apex court began to feel that it wasn't enough. In a progressive declaration that *only* physical contact should not be deemed sexual harassment – and that the latter's scope needed to be broadened to include several other verbal and non-verbal cues – the Supreme Court directed all states to come up with mechanisms to better carry out the Vishaka Guidelines. 'The implementation of the guidelines in Vishaka has to be not only in form, but substance and spirit, so as to make available safe and secure environment to women at the workplace in every aspect … The Court is of the considered view that *the existing laws, if necessary, be revised and appropriate new laws be enacted by Parliament and the State Legislatures* to protect women from any form of indecency, indignity and disrespect at all places.' (emphasis own).[7]

Despite the Supreme Court's consternation and its clear missive to the states to do better, the Indian government did not come up with legislation until 2013. But when it finally did, it codified a set of laws that, bowing before the Supreme Court's disapproval, included all the levels and layers of harassment that a woman employee could potentially face.

This law/Act – that superseded the Vishaka Guidelines – became the Prevention of Sexual Harassment at the Workplace Act (PoSHA).

Smita has been in a quandary for the past four years, oscillating between frequent self-flagellation and a palpable sense of injustice done to her that she's never known where to direct. Of the many survivors I've reported on – some of whose stories find place in this book – Smita, above all of them, has lacked an anchor, or just about anyone who'd tell her that it wasn't her fault and that they'll help her. If she had known that the state itself had had the wherewithal to help and yet, had failed her, systemically – through the machinations of an indifferent workplace, the inertia of a police system and the torpor of a court in summoning her to trial – would she have felt any better? Or only infinitely worse?

I cannot answer that. I only know that they collectively failed her, and that, born out of the lapses of a state, is the complete and utter breakdown of an individual's psyche.

The absence of any state mechanism, at any point, for Smita to harness, only led to her believing that she was without help *everywhere* else. Was she treated like an equal at the workplace? Doubtful. Did she believe herself to be an equal in relationships, therefore? Equally dubious.

Smita's stories are peppered with what is 'normal' to her – anecdotes of 'haath chhodna' and the liberal mapping of bruises on her flesh, or the lack, thereof, to calibrate the affection of a man who is with her. Not for her, the simple, the subtle, the layered and the innocuous. Smita's sex and love lives are governed by a dichotomy of black and white – the men who love her and the men who hit her or rape her. Sometimes, they are both the same man.

At the end of four years and two rapes, Smita's overwhelming concern has to do with inconveniencing nobody and shrinking herself to insignificance.

She should be very, very angry. Instead, she's beaten down.

What a monumental failure the state has wrought on her. At the end of four years.

And two rapes.

# Author's Note

THE NAMES OF ALL SURVIVORS AND THEIR FAMILY members have been changed throughout. The names of actual officials, police personnel, practising attorneys and NGO members who have been interviewed through the course of research for this book have been retained. No names or locations of exact villages or towns have been given, except to refer to a broad geographical region, for instance, 'northwestern Delhi', or a 'little way from Dewas, Madhya Pradesh' and others.

It took me a couple of years to finish writing this book. But in a sense, I started writing it decades ago and in a sense, the process of writing it still isn't over. The women who've consented to sharing their stories and opening their hearts out to me, to be consecrated in this book, know fully well that this isn't over.

Don't let their rapes die quiet deaths. Ask for more. Strip them of their shame and lay ignominy at the doors of those to whom it rightfully belongs: the men who rape. Ask for more: of a government, a justice system, of our indifference. Survivors do not possess the luxury of indifference, honed over years of righteous rage, piqued only by the correct cause at the appropriate time. Ask for more of homes where egalitarianism does not exist; of families where men grow to be entitled and women, frightened; of streets and nights whose gates are shut to one sex and open to others.

Then, rage, rage into the night.

# Acknowledgements

WHERE DO I EVEN BEGIN WITH THIS BOOK? TO ME, IT'S THE culmination of the years' worth of labour, love and luck – but, in many ways, I've been writing or building up to writing this for years. Thirty, to be precise. For that, I have my parents to thank. My mom and dad instilled a ferocious sense of social justice in me – as also the awareness of the inequities in our socio-economic spectrum. They also taught me to stand up for those who the system disadvantaged, while standing up against those who exploited their own advantage. They also give me unparalled love, comfort and respect – supporting me through everything I do and believing the best of me. I love you both so fiercely.

In that vein, I have my sister to thank, too. Older by only a couple of years, Didi was my first friend and is my strongest cheerleader. I know she'll be so proud when she picks up a copy of this book, and that assurance fills me with so much warmth.

My partner, Adi, who I live with, hugged me tight and held me close after many an excruciating phone call – often accompanying me to homes of children who had come to mean a lot to me, over the years. He offered empathy and righteous indignation, the allyship of a feminist and the advice of a man equally invested in eliminating social injustice – all of the reasons I love him, and more. I couldn't have asked for better support through the writing of something like this which often tore and gnawed at my insides, leaving me irrefutably changed.

I also couldn't thank the team at Pan Macmillan India enough – for trusting a book as raw and relevant as this one – but, particularly, my editor, Avneet Kaur. I remember the first time I met her, during what I assumed would be a run-of-the-mill tête-a-tête to discuss my writing/her editing processes – and how quickly that devolved into a mutual exchange of solidarity. 'It broke my heart,' she said simply of the manuscript she'd just read – now, two years ago – 'I had to put it down after a day, because it was so painful. But I returned, because I knew that pain was important to read.' If I've never told Avneet this, I should say so now: that understanding of the book and her kindness far outweighed anything procedural or editorial that she brought – albeit, equally exemplarily – to *After I Was Raped*.

My thanks are also due to Kanishka Gupta – my agent and literary agent extraordinaire – who works indefatigably and who reposed faith in me at a time I most needed it.

And then, there are the friends and the colleagues – old and new – the mentors and the teachers over the years, whose cheerleading and expertise, confidence-boosting and soul-nourishing qualities I am so thankful for today.

The biggest acknowledgements, of course, go to the people you have read about in the pages to come whose voices emanate from everything that you think is good about this book. I hope their stories spoke to you as much as they did to me – they could do with you in their corner.

# Notes

## Introduction: What Happens after Rape?

1. 'Out of 34,651 Rape Cases, in 33,098 Cases Offenders Were Known to the Victims Accounting for 95.5%(33,098 out of 34,651 Cases) of Total Rape Cases during 2015,' *Crime in India 2015: Compendium*, National Crime Records Bureau. Available at: https://ncrb.gov.in/sites/default/files/Compendium/Compendium-15.11.16.pdf.

## 1. Nidhi

1. *User Handbook on Protection of Children from Sexual Offences Act, 2012*, National Commission for Protection of Child Rights, September 2017. Available at: https://ncpcr.gov.in/showfile.php?lang=1&level=1&&sublinkid=1289&lid=1514.
2. *Model Guidelines under Section 39 of The Protection of Children from Sexual Offences Act, 2012*, Ministry of Women and Child Development, September 2013. Available at: https://wcd.nic.in/sites/default/files/POCSO-ModelGuidelines.pdf.
3. *User Handbook on Protection of Children from Sexual Offences Act, 2012*.

4. *Model Guidelines under Section 39, The Protection of Children from Sexual Offences Act, 2012.*

5. Ibid.

6. '96% of 1.7L Pending Rape Trials POCSO Cases; Govt Eyes 1,000 Special Courts,' *Times of India*, 12 July 2019. Available at: https://epaper.timesgroup.com/Olive/ODN/TimesOfIndia/shared/ShowArticle.

7. Ibid.

## 2. Meera

1. Jan Sahas, 'About Us.' Available at: https://jansahas.org/about-us.

2. Jayshree Bajoria, 'Doctors in India Continue to Traumatise Rape Survivors with the Two-Finger Test,' Human Rights Watch, 9 November 2017. Available at: https://www.hrw.org/news/2017/11/09/doctors-india-continue-traumatise-rape-survivors-two-finger-test.

3. Urmi Bhattacheryya, 'Sshh! Raped by Her Pundit, She Was Subjected to a Two-Finger Test'. *The Quint*, 3 June 2018. Available at: https://www.thequint.com/voices/women/rape-survivor-two-finger-test-banned-india-rapist-free.

4. *The Medical Examination of Survivors/Victims of Sexual Violence: A Handbook For Medical Officers,* United Nations Fund for Population Activities (UNFPA), Public Health Department and National Health Mission (NHM), 2017.

5. Ibid.

6. Jayshree Bajoria, '"Everyone Blames Me": Barriers to Justice and Support Services for Sexual Assault Survivors in India,' Human Rights Watch, 8 November 2017.

7. Aruna Kashyap, Reena Reddy and Fussell Chloë, *Dignity on Trial: India's Need for Sound Standards for Conducting and Interpreting Forensic Examinations of Rape Survivors* (New York: Human Rights Watch, 2010). Available at: https://www.hrw.org/sites/default/files/reports/india0910webwcover.pdf.
8. PTI, 'No Two-finger Test for Rape: Supreme Court,' *Hindu*, 19 May 2013. Available at: https://www.thehindu.com/news/national/No-two-finger-test-for-rape-SC/article12141055.ece.

## 4. Caste and Sexual Assault

1. *National Crime Records Bureau.* Available at: https://ncrb.gov.in/en/directors-desk.
2. *Crime in India 2015*, National Crime Records Bureau, 2016.
3. *Crime in India 2020*, National Crime Records Bureau, 2021.
4. 'India: Authorities Must Impartially Investigate Gang-rape and Murder of Dalit Girls,' Amnesty International, 30 May 2014. Available at: https://www.amnesty.org/en/latest/news/2014/05/india-authorities-must-impartially-investigate-gang-rape-and-murder-dalit-girls/.
5. Ibid.
6. Ismat Ara, 'Hathras Gang-Rape and Murder Case: A Timeline,' *Wire*, 28 October 2020. Available at: https://thewire.in/women/hathras-gang-rape-and-murder-case-a-timeline.
7. 'Madhya Pradesh Shocker: Raped for Months, Dalit Woman Carries Aborted Fetus to Police to Lodge Case

against Tormentors,' *New Indian Express*, 6 April 2018. Available at: https://www.newindianexpress.com/nation/2018/apr/06/madhya-pradesh-shocker-raped-for-months-dalit-woman-carries-aborted-fetus-to-police-to-lodge-case-1797592.html.

8. 'Badaun Gangrape and Murder: How the Incident Unfolded,' *Indian Express*, 2 June 2014. Available at: https://indianexpress.com/article/india/india-others/badaun-gangrape-and-murder-how-the-incident-unfolded.

9. 'Baghpat "Khap Diktat": UP Police Can Probe Rape Case,' *Indian Express*, 17 September 2015. Available at: https://indianexpress.com/article/india/india-others/baghpat-khap-diktat-up-police-can-probe-rape-case.

10. Urmi Bhattacheryya, 'How Mother-Daughter Have Been Locked in a Battle Against Rape,' *The Quint*, 18 March 2019. Available at: https://www.thequint.com/neon/gender/minor-rape-survivor-and-mother-wait-for-justice.

11. Bajoria, '"Everyone Blames Me",' Human Rights Watch.

12. Ibid.

## 5. Pia

1. Swati Maliwal, Twitter, 29 January 2018, 10:39 p.m. Available at: https://twitter.com/SwatiJaiHind/status/958024309322211328.

2. Indo-Asian News Service, 'Supreme Court Directs AIIMS Doctors to Supervise Rape Case of 8-month-old Girl,' *India Today*, 31 January 2018. Available at: https://www.indiatoday.in/india/story/supreme-court-directs-aiims-doctors-to-supervise-rape-case-of-8-month-old-girl-1158578-2018-01-31.

## 6. Smita

1. Section 164, *The Code Of Criminal Procedure*, 1973. Available at: https://indiankanoon.org/doc/497457/.
2. Sofi Annan, 'Bail for Rape: High Court Blames Victim for "Mindset",' *Indian Express*, 22 September 2017. Available at: https://indianexpress.com/article/india/bail-for-rape-high-court-blames-victim-for-her-mindset-4855374/.
3. *The Indian Evidence (Amendment) Act, 2002*. Available at: https://indiankanoon.org/doc/1555515/.
4. *The Sexual Harassment of Women at Workplace (Prevention, Prohibition and Redressal) Act, 2013*, Ministry of Law and Justice, April 2013.
5. Geeta Pandey, 'Bhanwari Devi: The Rape That Led to India's Sexual Harassment Law,' *BBC*, 17 March 2017.
6. *Vishaka and Others Versus State of Rajasthan and Others*, The Supreme Court of India, 13 August 1997. Available at: https://www.iiap.res.in/files/VisakaVsRajasthan_1997.pdf.
7. *Medha Kotwal Lele and Others Versus Union of India and Others*, The Supreme Court of India, 19 October 2012.